THE HISTORY OF VERMONT

FROM ITS EARLIEST SETTLEMENT TO THE PRESENT TIME

W. H. CARPENTER
T. S. ARTHUR

Published by Left of Brain Books

Copyright © 2021 Left of Brain Books

ISBN 978-1-396-32009-5

First Edition

Table of Contents

PREFACE.

THE present History of Vermont is from the pen of a gentleman whose fine literary abilities have often been favourably acknowledged by the public. It has been written expressly for this Cabinet series of State Histories, and, like the volumes which have preceded it, is wholly original.

The responsibility of perfect accuracy rests upon those whose names are on the title page; the only duty devolving upon them, in this instance, having been that of careful collation with the original authorities.

CHAPTER I.

THE long and irregular lake which forms the western boundary of the State of Vermont, bears the name of the European who earliest explored any portion of its territory, Samuel Champlain, the first successful founder of French settlements in North America. He was for many years the governor of New France, as the French Canadian possessions were called; and he has left behind him a monument which has survived the last trace of French dominion on this continent. He published a curious work entitled "Voyages and Travels in New France," or Canada. It possessed sufficient interest to call for a modern reprint; and in 1838, more than two hundred years from its first appearance, was republished in Paris.

Champlain's observations on the aborigines were so exact that his successors have in few cases found reason to depart from his conclusions. Perhaps we should except such writers as invest the American Indian with imaginary traits of impossible heroism, and with savage virtues of a higher than the civilized standard. He records a very minute account of their shocking barbarities to their prisoners, of which he was, most probably, the first European witness. And he gives us relations of their garrulity and nimble-tongued vituperations and rejoinders, which contrast very strongly with the dramatic Indian, reserved and dignified. He describes hostile Indian nations making ready for a fight at dawn by dancing in hearing of each other, and preparing themselves for the encounter by a whole night of mutual reviling; and when, by the aid of European strategy, he had enabled an Indian besieging force to take a position commanding the enemy's entrenchment, the martial Frenchman was astonished to find the siege delayed while the combatants hurled curses at each other.

From various causes the French coalesced with the Indians better than any other colonists have done. There was less repugnance of race and caste between them. And the wisdom of the Jesuits, who were effective leaders in all French intercourse with the Indians, procured a clause in the charters which performed wonders for French enterprise. Every convert, upon baptism, became *ipso facto* a French subject. He was entitled to equal privileges with the colonists. He was identified with their success, and bound to them by much stronger ties than the subsidies of the English could ever purchase. Whatever may be charged against the Jesuits, their heroism and self-denial cannot be gain-said; and, without entering into a discussion of the matter of their teaching as compared with that of the Protestant missionaries, they certainly made firmer temporal allies of their Indian converts.

With all his sagacity, Champlain's love of adventure led him into a capital error; a mistake which did not cease to operate until the French were entirely dispossessed of Canada. He sought a north-west passage to Cathay—a problem which, even unto the present day, promotes incidental benefits to commerce and geographical knowledge, without any approach to its own solution. The error to which we refer, was that of espousing the quarrel of one Indian tribe or family of tribes against another. The Indians who held the lands on the Atlantic were the Algonquins. From Lake Champlain, as far west as Huron, the warlike Iroquois, sometimes called the Six Nations, were in possession. Champlain, on condition of being guided through the territories of these fierce tribes, readily undertook to aid the Algonquins in their wars against them. His visit to Lake Champlain and Lake George, which took place in 1609, was made under such unlucky auspices; and the first knowledge which the Iroquois had of the French was as the allies of their hereditary enemies. Three Frenchmen only appear to have been present, but their arquebuses decided the day in favour of the Algonquins; and this commencement entailed persecution and death upon many an unfortunate missionary, and provoked the Iroquois to adhesion to the Dutch and English in New York.

Vermont was not in the path to Cathay, and the French seem to have paid little heed to the territory of the future fourteenth state in the American confederacy. The French missionaries and explorers were confined to the north of the St. Lawrence, and north and west of the Lakes Erie and Ontario.

They were in friendly relations with the Indians near Lake Superior, while they could not venture upon the Ontario or Erie; and their unceasing wars with the Mohawks forced their missionaries to run the gauntlet through fierce tribes before they could reach their stations near Lake Huron. These Mohawks were Iroquois, the tribe whose first acquaintance with the French we have mentioned as derived from their fire-arms, which scattered death in a new and wonderful manner.

Lake Champlain divided the country of the Iroquois and the Algonquins. Its waters, as they had been before Champlain saw them, still remained the highway of war parties for nearly two hundred years. Vermont west of the mountains was uninhabitable. Even the savages avoided it for any purpose of permanent residence; and it merited the name which has been given to another portion of our continent, "The Dark and Bloody Ground." English and French expeditions followed the old war-paths, guided by savage allies; and the Hudson River and Lakes George and Champlain seemed practically useful only as military avenues. In 1760, when the French lost Canada, this state of things ceased; but Lake Champlain was again the scene of hostilities during the revolutionary period, and during the second war between the United States and Great Britain.

It does not come within our scope to give the details of the murderous Indian conflicts of which the territory of Vermont was the theatre before its settlement. Many of these events belong to the history of another state, and are there treated. The first permanent settlement in Vermont was made in 1724, in its southeastern corner, on the land now embraced within the town of Brattleborough. This post was called Fort Dummer, and was supposed to be within the jurisdiction of Massachusetts. The French, in 1731, made a settlement on Lake Champlain, within the limits of the present town of Addison. They also established on the opposite or New York shore, a fortress which they called St. Frederick, but which was afterward known as Crown Point. In 1759, Crown Point and the settlements on the Vermont side were abandoned by the French, who retreated to Canada before the victorious arms of Lord Amherst. No European settlements now remained in Vermont, except a few in the southeast corner, which had been undertaken under the protection of New Hampshire. The land still remained in its primeval wilderness. But a military road from Charlestown, in New Hampshire, to

Crown Point, crossing the territory of the present State of Vermont, had apprized the public of the character and value of the land; and when the French war was ended, in 1760, there were abundance of applicants for tracts. Vermont, so long closed to emigrants, now became a land of promise, and population flowed toward it with what was then considered great rapidity. The spirit of the hostile Indians had been subdued by several exemplary inflictions, the ferocity of which can only be excused by the exasperation which the borderers felt against a ruthless foe, with whom no argument except force seemed to avail.

CHAPTER II.

Boundary line between Massachusetts and New Hampshire established — New Hampshire required to support Fort Dummer — Township grants by the governor of New Hampshire — Bennington founded — Claims of New York — Number of grants issued — Fees for the same — Controversy with New York — Duke of York's patent — Its vagueness — Cadwallader Colden of New York — His proclamation — Counter-proclamation from New Hampshire — Eastern boundary of New York defined by England — Jurisdiction asserted over Vermont — The grants from New Hampshire declared null and void — Resistance by the people — Their appeal to the British ministry — Royal orders to New York — Writs of ejectment obtained — Inability to execute them — Land speculators — Hatred of them in Vermont — Ethan Allen — His character — The Green Mountain Boys.

THE impediments to the success of the infant state did not cease with the close of Indian hostilities. In the year 1740, to put a period to the controversy between Massachusetts and New Hampshire respecting the boundary between them, the British government established a line parallel with the Merrimack River, at three miles distance, from the Atlantic to Pawtucket Falls, and thence due west to the boundary of New York. This line, while it settled the controversy between Massachusetts and New Hampshire, opened another dispute, which lasted for a quarter of a century. Fort Dummer, and the few settlements west of the Connecticut were found by this line not to be in Massachusetts. The King of Great Britain repeatedly called upon the New Hampshire legislature to make provision for the support of Fort Dummer. The presumption grew up that the jurisdiction of New Hampshire extended west as far as that of Massachusetts; that is to say, to a line twenty miles east from Hudson River.

In 1749, Benning Wentworth, Governor of New Hampshire, made a grant of a township six miles square, situated, as he conceived, on the western borders of New Hampshire, being twenty miles east of the Hudson River, and six miles north of the Massachusetts line. This township he called Bennington. He granted also fifteen other townships; but the breaking out of hostilities

6

between England and France put a stop to applications. A correspondence had meanwhile arisen between the governors of New Hampshire and New York, in which the latter, under an old grant from Charles II. to the Duke of York, claimed all the land west of the Connecticut River. As, however, this grant would have covered the lands in Massachusetts and Connecticut west of the river, and no claim had been established against those provinces, the governor of New Hampshire paid no heed to the pretensions of New York.

After the close of the French war, in 1760, the governor of New Hampshire resumed the granting of townships, and in the course of two or three years issued grants to the number of one hundred and ninety-eight. The fees on each were about one hundred dollars. In each township he reserved five hundred acres for himself, and in this mode he accumulated a large fortune. These perquisites were emoluments which New York was determined not tamely to relinquish, and a war of proclamations forthwith commenced. Although for convenience we have used the name Vermont, and shall continue to do so, the name was not as yet applied to the territory. The people styled themselves the inhabitants of the "New Hampshire Grants."

Whatever might be said of the claims of New Hampshire to jurisdiction, that of New York was vague and indefensible. In the first place, the grant to the Duke of York was very indefinite, as were most of the parcellings out of this continent by European powers. It gave the Duke of York "all the lands from the west side of the Connecticut River to the east side of the Delaware Bay," a boundary, the vagueness of which we need not enlarge upon. But whatever title it might have conferred upon the Duke of York was merged in the crown upon James's accession, and descended to William upon James's abdication; so that the authority of the royal governor of New Hampshire was quite as good under this very grant as that of New York. It established no colony and authorized no government; and the Massachusetts and Connecticut charters were given without regard to the previous royal disposal of "all the lands" west of the Connecticut.

Nevertheless the perquisites which accrued from land grants could not be willingly given up by New York; and in 1763, Cadwallader Colden, acting governor of that province, issued his proclamation reciting the obsolete grant to the Duke of York, and claiming jurisdiction as far as the Connecticut River. He also commanded the sheriff of Albany to make returns of the names of all persons who had taken up lands under grants from New Hampshire. In reply, the governor of New Hampshire issued his proclamation, denying the validity of the old grant under which New York claimed, and asserting the western limits of New Hampshire to be a continuation northerly of the western line of Connecticut and Massachusetts. He told the settlers that their claims to their lands under the New Hampshire grants would be unaffected, even though they should come under the jurisdiction of New York. He exhorted the people to be industrious and diligent, and to proceed without intimidation to cultivate their territory; and he commanded the civil officers to exercise jurisdiction as far as the grants extended. The ground taken by the governor of New Hampshire in this proclamation, in regard to land titles, was not only plausible but equitable. It could not be supposed that a dispute about jurisdiction between two royal governors could vitiate the grants which either had made, as a representative of the crown. The minds of the people were quieted, and no fears for the future were entertained.

The New York authorities, convinced perhaps of the untenable nature of their claims, or willing to put them on a clearer basis, even while they were defending the obsolete grant to the Duke of York, were operating in England to obtain a less questionable title. They procured in 1764 a decision by the British crown that the Connecticut River, from the Massachusetts line to the forty-fifth degree of north latitude, should be the eastern boundary of New York. The application for this decree based the request on the "convenience and advantage of the people;" and it was more than suspected that it was supported by a fraudulent use of the names of the settlers, who were those most interested.

The decree, or the mode in which it was obtained, was not at first subjected to any rigid examination, or made the subject of any complaint. The people were rather pleased than otherwise that the troublesome question of jurisdiction was determined; and imagined that their titles would be confirmed by it, rather than impaired. They supposed the decree would have an entirely prospective action; and were alarmed and astonished when the New York authorities gave it a retrospective interpretation, and claimed that it vitiated the grants from New Hampshire. The government of New York proceeded under this interpretation to declare the titles given by New Hampshire null and void, and to require the settlers to take out new grants from New York, and to surrender their New Hampshire charters. Aside from the injustice in principle of this demand, it was accompanied with onerous pecuniary conditions; for, whereas, the modest province of New Hampshire had been content with fees amounting to only one hundred dollars on each township, New York claimed from two thousand to twenty-six hundred. The New Hampshire grants were divided into four new counties, and courts were held in them under the new jurisdiction. Some few of the towns complied with the hard terms, and bought their lands over again. But the greater number of townships refused to submit to what they justly deemed a gross and cruel imposition. Where the people refused to submit, fresh grants were made of their lands, and suits were commenced in the names of the new grantees, for the ejectment of the original holders. There was no difficulty in obtaining judgments against the settlers, but there was no possibility of enforcing them. The people banded together for mutual support; and the officers met with such rough treatment that few dared, at length, to present themselves for the performance of a duty so odious. The people were left without redress in the ordinary forms of law; and even the governor of New Hampshire felt compelled, though unwillingly, to issue his proclamation recommending the settlers on the grants to yield due obedience to the laws and authority of New York.

The settlers associated themselves together; and held frequent conventions to devise means of resisting the wrongs which were attempted against them. As the governor of New York had appealed to the British government, the "Green Mountain Boys," as they now began to be called, determined to make an effort to be heard there also, nothing doubting that a true representation of their case would be followed by measures for their relief. The result justified their expectations, so far as the will of the British crown was concerned. The Lords of the Board of Trade and Plantations having investigated the subject in 1767, the governor of New York received the following order: "His majesty doth hereby strictly charge, require, and command, that the governor or commander-in-chief of his majesty's province of New York, for the time being, do not, upon pain of his majesty's highest displeasure, presume to make any grants whatsoever, of any part of the land described, until his majesty's further pleasure shall be known concerning the same."

This royal mandate was certainly explicit and satisfactory enough, so far as its apparent meaning and intention could be gathered from its plain English. But whether "his majesty's further pleasure" was immediately communicated to the New York governor, revoking this order, or whether the governor found the fees too lucrative to be tamely surrendered, the people soon found that royal orders gave them no respite. No regard was paid to the royal mandate. New grants continued to be made, and actions of ejectment continued to be pressed in the courts at Albany. The Green Mountain Boys paid no heed to these proceedings, and suffered judgment to go against them by default. They complained, and with reason, that the officers of New York, while calling upon the people to obey the royal orders and decisions, violated those injunctions themselves.

The militia were called in to aid and support the sheriff and his officers. But this measure served only to demonstrate the weakness of a government which aimed to enforce the perpetration of a wrong. The claimants holding titles purchased under such circumstances had not a feeling in common with the people. They were speculators, odious for the fact that they would attempt to possess themselves of what was the equitable property of others. They were loathed as adventurers who preferred an unjust course, rather than to purchase lands at a fair valuation to which there was no adverse claims—idlers, who would willingly derive emolument from the distress of the hardy pioneers who had subdued the forest. The militia, when summoned, though compelled to march, had no affection for the business, and declined hazarding their lives against their convictions, and against the people with whom they sympathized, for the emolument of speculators for whom they had no respect. Wherever a show of opposition was made, the New York militia refused to act; and the sheriff with his posse were in a worse predicament than without it. The exasperation of the people was increased, and the fugitive posse only emboldened the resistants.

The name of Ethan Allen, celebrated in connection with the Revolutionary war, appears first in the history of these struggles of the people of the New Hampshire grants against their grasping neighbours. Allen was born in Litchfield, Connecticut, but emigrated with his parents to the New Hampshire grants at an early age. He possessed in a rare degree that indispensable requisite to a self-constituted leader in troublous times—rude and overbearing self-confidence. He was abashed by no consciousness of ignorance, and made boldness in the declaration of his opinions serve him in the place of a more refined style. As the right was manifestly on his side, and he vigorously contended against an injustice, the effects of which he suffered under in common with others, the leadership to which his daring impetuosity made him aspire was at once accorded to him. There was at this time no newspaper in Vermont, and, indeed, no printing office; but Ethan Allen entered vigorously into the contest with New York as a pamphleteer. He was the author of the manifestoes of the Green Mountain Boys, to which, with other names, his was appended.

Allen's method of expression in these appeals to the public was in keeping with the character of the public which he addressed. They can scarce be read now without a smile, their inkshed being of the most ferocious character. The rude borderers of that day found their own feelings well represented in the harsh language of Allen. Their all was at stake, and no terms seemed too severe to denounce their oppressors. If the better educated among them perceived, as they doubtless did, the absurdity of the pamphleteer, they were too politic to take exception to what seemed best adapted to keep up that excitement, which alone promised successful and continued resistance. The nature of the population of the New Hampshire grants is thus summed by Dr. Samuel Williams, the first historian of Vermont:—

"The main body of the settlers at that time, consisted of a brave, hardy, intrepid, but uncultivated set of men. Without many of the advantages of education, without any other property than what hard labour and hard living had procured, destitute of the conveniences and the elegancies of life, and having nothing to soften or refine their manners, roughness, excess, and violence would naturally mark their proceedings. To deny such people justice was to prejudice and arm them against it; to confirm all those suspicions and prejudices against their rulers, and to give them an excuse and plea to proceed to outrage and violence. When the government of New York gave to these proceedings the names of mobs and riots, abuse and outrage, it is probable that such expressions conveyed pretty just ideas of the appearance of their conduct and opposition to the laws. But when they called their opposition treason, felony, and rebellion against lawful authority, the people of the adjoining provinces seem to have believed that the government of New York was much more blamable in making and exercising such laws as called these titles to their lands in question, than the settlers were in acting in open and avowed opposition to them."

CHAPTER III.

The Green Mountain Tavern — Its sign — Convention at Bennington — Determination of the settlers — Organized opposition to New York — Committees of Safety formed — Military associations — Indictment of Allen, Warner, and others — Rewards offered for their apprehension — Attempted arrest of Warner — Conciliatory efforts of Governor Tryon — Exception of the ringleaders — Proclamations and counter-proclamations — Decree of the Green Mountain Convention — Green Mountain law — The Beech Seal — Action of the New York Assembly — General convention west of the Green Mountains — Resolutions adopted — Sanguinary laws of New York — Respouse of the Mountaineers — Colonel Skeen's mission to England — Approach of the Revolution.

BENNINGTON, the first town chartered by the Governor of New Hampshire, was one of the chief rallying places of the Green Mountain Boys. The "Green Mountain Tavern" in this village had a sign expressive of the defiance of the settlers. On the very borders of the disputed territory, a post twenty-five feet high bore on its top a huge catamount's skin, stuffed, its teeth displayed toward the hated province of New York. One mode of punishing any traitor to the Green Mountain interest, was to hoist him, tied in an arm chair, up to the sign, and let him hang one hour or more, according to the pleasure of his judges, exposed to the mocking of the crowd which such an occasion did not fail to summon.

After the refusal of the authorities of New York to heed the royal mandate forbidding new grants, a convention of the settlers was called at Bennington; and at this convention it was "resolved to support the rights and property which they possessed under the New Hampshire grants, against the usurpation and unjust claims of the governor and council of New York, by force, as law and justice were denied them." Opposition took now an organized and formidable character. "Committees of Safety" were appointed in most of the towns west of the Green Mountains; and these committees took cognizance of matters within their several precincts, or in convention passed resolutions and decrees which had the force of law over the settlers. A military

13

association was formed, of which Ethan Allen was appointed colonel, and Seth Warner and five others captains. The authorities of New York proceeded to cause the leaders in these movements to be indicted as rioters; and the governor of that province issued a proclamation offering one hundred and fifty pounds sterling, or six hundred and sixty-six dollars, for the apprehension of Colonel Allen; and fifty pounds, or two hundred and twenty-two dollars, for each of the others. Allen then issued his proclamation, offering five pounds, rather more than twenty-two dollars, to any person who would apprehend the attorney-general of the colony of New York, and deliver him to any officer of the Green Mountain Boys. An officer of New York, moved perhaps by the reward, visited the grants with the purpose of arresting Warner. The Green Mountain captain gave him battle, wounded and disarmed him, but spared the life which was at his mercy. Indeed, through all the scenes of violence which attended the efforts of New York to enforce unjust and unpopular laws, the resistants avoided any sanguinary acts, though their proclamations had a ferocious sound. They gave fair warning of their intentions, and warned the offenders against their decrees to desist. Persistence in spite of warning was rigorously punished, after due examination had before a committee of safety.

Efforts were made in 1772, by Governor Tryon of New York, to conciliate. But his overtures excepted Allen and some others, and the negotiations were interrupted by the proceedings of exasperated parties. Certain settlers, who occupied lands under grants from New York, were dispossessed and driven away by the Green Mountain Boys; and when the New York governor required the lands to be restored, the settlers called a convention, and drew up a report, declining compliance with the governor's mandate, and vindicating their proceedings. Negotiations here terminated; and the governor, council, and legislature of New York, on the one hand, and the Green Mountain Boys on the other, proceeded to the fulmination of proclamations, and the enactment of decrees and laws, which lacked only power to enforce them, to revive the worst scenes of the worst despotism. Happily their fury was expended in ink and evaporated in bravado.

The Green Mountain convention decreed that no person should take grants or confirmations of grants under the government of New York. It forbade all the inhabitants of the New Hampshire grants to hold, take, or accept any office of honour or profit under the colony of New York; and all civil and military officers who had acted under such authority were commanded to suspend their functions. The penalty for neglect or refusal was "being *viewed*" by a committee of safety. What "viewing" implied may be gathered from the case of one Benjamin Hough, who presumed to act under a New York commission as a justice of the peace, after warning given him to desist.

The culprit was arrested and brought before the committee of safety at Sunderland. When interrogated, he pleaded the jurisdiction and authority of the province of New York. He was answered by the decree of the convention above referred to, of which no settler on the grants could be ignorant. And the committee proceeded to pass the following sentence, which was summarily carried into execution: "That the prisoner be taken from the bar of this committee of safety, and tied to a tree, and there on his naked back receive one hundred stripes. His back being dressed, he shall depart out of the district, and on his return, unless by special leave of the committee, he shall suffer death."

The instruments with which flagellation was inflicted were "twigs of the wilderness;" and this mode of punishment was termed, by the Green Mountain Boys, the application of the "beech seal." Where the validity of the great seal of the province of New Hampshire was not considered sufficient by the adherents of New York, it was quaintly intimated that the "beech seal" upon their naked backs would be regarded by them as abundant confirmation.

These measures, of course, exasperated the New York authorities. The settlers on the New Hampshire grants, west of the mountains, who were in collision with the New York authorities, were denounced as lawless banditti. Their proceedings were characterized as treason and rebellion; and, powerless as New York had proved to enforce former enactments, she made the common mistake of adding to former acts, which remained dead letters, new enactments as inoperative in effect as they were Draco-like in spirit. A committee of the assembly reported a series of resolutions upon the proceedings of the "Bennington Mob," in which they desired his excellency, the governor, to offer a reward for the securing of the ringleaders, and their committal to Albany jail. And they recommended that a law should be passed "more effectually to suppress riotous proceedings, and bring the offenders to condign punishment."

15

These preliminary proceedings having transpired, a general convention of the inhabitants of the western townships was held on the 1st of March, 1774, and adjourned to the third Wednesday in that month. At this meeting a report was adopted giving a review of past events, and recommending the New York authorities to wait the determination of his majesty before proceeding to further extremities. It concluded with resolutions, among which were the following: "That, as a country, we will stand by and defend our friends and neighbours who are indicted, at the expense of our lives and fortunes;" and "that for the future, every necessary preparation be made, and that our inhabitants hold themselves in readiness, at a minute's warning, to aid and defend such friends of ours who, for their merit in the great and general cause, are falsely denominated rioters; but that we will not act anything, more or less than on the defensive, and also encourage due execution of law in civil cases, and also in criminal prosecutions that are so indeed; and also that we will assist, to the utmost of our power, the officers appointed for that purpose."

It will be noted that the above resolutions still held out the hope of accommodation. But the New York legislature, influenced perhaps by the speculators, and irritated by the disposition of the settlers under New York grants, proceeded to pass a law in accordance with the resolutions of their committee. Governor Tryon was absent in England, whither he had repaired to lay the difficulties which he encountered before the royal government; and Cadwallader Colden, at that time very old, was acting governor of the province. The law which the wisdom of New York devised was a curiosity in American legislation. Whether it ever could have received the sanction of the crown is doubtful; nor do we know with what propositions for the settlement of the difficulty Governor Tryon returned to America; for on his arrival, which did not take place until 1775, he found more engrossing and important business than the quarrels of land-jobbers with the Green Mountain Boys.

The territory west of the Green Mountains, in which the malecontents principally resided, was divided into two parts, one of which formed the county of Charlotte, and the other was annexed to Albany. The new law applied exclusively to those counties. It enacted that if any person opposed a civil officer of New York in the discharge of his official duty, or willingly burned or destroyed property, or being riotously assembled proceeded unlawfully to the destruction of buildings, such offences should be adjudged felony without benefit of clergy, and the offenders should suffer death as felons. It made it the duty of the governor to publish in the public papers, and to cause to be affixed in public places by the sheriffs, the names of any persons indicted for capital offences, with an order commanding the surrender of themselves within seventy days. In case of their non-appearance within the seventy days they were to be adjudged guilty, and the courts might award execution against them in the same manner as if they had been convicted, and death be inflicted without benefit of clergy. All crimes committed on the New Hampshire grants were by this act permitted to be tried by the courts of the county of Albany; and the neglect to obey the summons to surrender themselves was equivalent to conviction. By this law the dangerous duty of serving process on the Green Mountain Boys was sought to be evaded, and they were summoned to appear for trial, or convict themselves by refusal.

At the same time a new proclamation was issued, offering a reward of fifty pounds, or two hundred and twenty-two dollars, each for apprehending Ethan Allen, Seth Warner, and six others who were regarded as the most prominent leaders among the malecontents. The effect of these measures was what might have been anticipated. The acknowledgment which the terms of the law virtually made, that New York was unable to enforce it, caused the measure and its abettors to be looked upon with contempt; and nerved the resistants to a fixed determination to meet death rather than submit. Past experience had convinced them that the people of New York had no desire to support the government, and the conduct of the New York militia had shown how little disposed their fellow-citizens were to aid the officers. The Green Mountain Boys gained in the moral strength which is conferred by public sympathy, and the ferocious sign of the Bennington hostelry glared still upon their oppressors.

Indeed, that sign furnished no inapt emblem of the whole business. Just as were the claims of the mountaineers, an air of solemn farce seems mingled with their proceedings, as we, secure in our rights, look back upon their wrongs and their strange manifestoes of defiance. If the law above noticed was a marvel in its way, the answer of the mountaineers, in convention adopted, was no less remarkable. It outheroded Herod.

It denounced in language which evinced a determination to be very severe, the character of the land-jobbers and their government, and thus depicted their doings:—"By legerdemain, bribery, and deception, they have extended their dominions far and wide. They have wrangled with, and encroached upon the neighbouring governments, and have used all manner of deceit and fraud to accomplish their designs. Their tenants groan under their usury and oppression; and they have gained as well as merited the disapprobation and abhorrence of their neighbours. The innocent blood they have already shed, calls for Heaven's vengeance on their guilty heads; and if they should come forth in arms against us, thousands of their injured neighbours will join with us to cut off and exterminate such an execrable race of men from the face of the earth.

"We, therefore," says the manifesto, "advertise such officers, and all persons whatsoever, that we are resolved to inflict *immediate death* on whomsoever shall attempt the apprehension of the persons indicted as rioters. And provided any of us, or our party, shall be taken, and we have not sufficient notice to relieve them, or whether we relieve them or not, we are resolved to surround such person or persons as shall take them, whether at his or their own house or houses, or any where that we can find him or them, and *shoot such person or persons dead*. And furthermore, we will *kill* and *destroy* any person or persons whomsoever, that shall presume to be accessory, aiding or assisting in taking any of us as aforesaid; for, by these presents, we give any such disposed person or persons to understand, that although they have a license by the law aforesaid to *kill us*, and an indemnification for such murder from the same authority, yet they have no indemnification for so doing from the *Green Mountain Boys*, for our lives, liberties, and properties are as verily precious to us as to any of the king's subjects. But if the governmental authority of New York insists upon killing us, to take possession of our vineyards, let them come on; we are ready for a game of scalping with them; for our martial spirits glow with bitter indignation and consummate fury to blast their infernal projects."

It does not appear that any collision occurred between the parties who had fulminated such furious threats against each other. The absence of Governor Tryon may have had some influence in preventing the parties from proceeding to extremities. Other steps were in progress to allay the difficulty. Colonel Philip Skeen, an English officer, who owned large tracts on Lake Champlain, went to England with a view to obtain the erection of a new province out of the Hampshire grants. He had the countenance of many of the inhabitants; and made some progress in his mission, for he wrote to a friend that he had been appointed governor of Crown Point and Ticonderoga. It is much to be regretted that this step had not been earlier taken, that it might have been perfected before the breaking out of hostilities between the colonies and the mother country. That event nipped Colonel Skeen's plan in the bud; but the future state of Vermont, established after much dispute, was the carrying out of his plan. Had it been consummated before the war, there would have been fourteen states in the original American confederation.

CHAPTER IV

The tenure of the royal judges in the colonies — Governor Hutchinson and the Massachusetts legislature — Petition for the removal of Chief Justice Oliver — His impeachment — Oliver sustained by Hutchinson — Appointment of counsellors by the crown — The opening of the Massachusetts courts of law obstructed by the people — Sympathy of the Green Mountain Boys — Possession taken of Westminster court house — Its surrender demanded by the sheriff of New York — The building fired into — Subsequent disposal of the prisoners — Westminster convention renounce the government of New York — Colonial disputes with Great Britain — Battle of Lexington — Population of Vermont — War of the Revolution.

THE events which we have narrated took place principally, if not entirely, on the western side of the Green Mountains. The inhabitants of that district were more exposed than their eastern neighbours to contact with the New York authorities. As a border population, with the hardihood and courage of frontier life, has also its rudeness and rough essentials, and as the western pioneers of Vermont had provocations which might well have influenced men of higher culture, we are not to wonder at their fierce and furious resolutions and manifestoes, or to be surprised at their summary application of forest law.

But while the inhabitants of the townships nearer New Hampshire remained comparatively inactive, it is not to be supposed that they lacked sympathy with the men upon whom fell the brunt of the encounter. And although some of the townships near the Connecticut River repurchased their grants, it was done with a tacit if not with a verbal protest. The injustice was felt; and when the time arrived for action the eastern settlers showed that they were not insensible to wrong, or disposed always to submit to what they regarded as tyranny.

The question of the tenure of the offices of the judges in the provincial courts was mooted in Massachusetts before the outbreak of hostilities. The point on which issue was joined was the manner in which their salaries should be paid. To render the governor and the judiciary independent of the people, provision was made for the payment of their salaries from England, or by the commissioners of the revenue from the customs' receipts. The mode had hitherto been to vote their salaries in the house of representatives; and the people resolutely refused to submit to the change. The governor they could not reach, except by indirect acts of retaliation; and these they felt justified in, since it was upon his suggestion, that the change was made. At the session of the legislature in 1772, when Governor Hutchinson declined to receive his salary from the province, he asked that the Province House, which had been often used as a residence for the chief magistrate, should be repaired and put in order for the reception of his family. The legislature replied that the building was intended for the governor of the province, who had heretofore received his support by order of the colonial legislature, but as Governor Hutchinson declined a salary offered by the province, and chose to be supported by the British government, they did not feel obliged to be at any charge for his accommodation. On a subsequent occasion, when the governor proposed to give a public dinner to the commissioners of the revenue, the people of Boston, in town meeting assembled, voted that if he desired Faneuil Hall for that purpose he should not have it.

But with the judges a more direct course was pursued. The house requested them to decline receiving their salaries from England. Three of them complied, and expressed their readiness to receive it from the province as heretofore. But Mr. Oliver, the chief justice, said he did not dare to decline it, without leave first obtained from the king. The house thereupon voted him unfit to hold the office of judge, and prayed the governor to remove him. The governor refused to act in the premises, alleging that the power of removal belonged to the crown. The house then proceeded to impeach Judge-Oliver of high crimes and misdemeanors, but the governor still refused to act. The people then in several of the counties, refused to take the usual oaths as grand jurors, when the courts were in session, until assured that the obnoxious judge would not be present. Another difficulty soon arose. Some of the judges were appointed to the council, as the upper branch of the legislature was then called; the crown assuming the right of appointing counsellors, whereas they had hitherto been elected by the house. The people of Boston regularly drawn, refused to act as jurors, but the panel was filled otherwise, and the business proceeded. At this stage of the contest, in some of the inland counties, the judges and officers were prevented from occupying the court houses—the people blocking up the entrances, and by sheer dead weight and pre-occupation, keeping them out. No forcible entry was attempted, and the delay of judicial action was submitted to by the obnoxious judges.

The pulse of the other New England colonies beat with Massachusetts. Vermont was settled chiefly by emigrants from Massachusetts, New Hampshire, and Connecticut; men who, from their adventurous spirit, would have an alacrity of resistance to oppression; and who, in the contests of the two royal governors of New Hampshire and New York had been sufferers in fact, while the governors suffered in dignity. The oppressive acts of New York would have made them resistants had all the rest of New England been loyal; and we are not, therefore, to wonder that the example of Massachusetts in relation to the obnoxious judges in that province, found ready imitators in the New Hampshire grants. The royal authority was suspended, after the continental congress of 1774, in nearly all the colonies, New York and Georgia alone withholding their formal sanction to the doings of the congress. In the latter province, the personal influence of the governor restrained the legislature from overt adhesion. In New York the loyalists were numerous, and the legislature was a moderate or "compromise body." Though petitions and addresses were adopted, similar in tone to the doings of the continental congress, the province nominally maintained its loyalty, after the other provinces, except Georgia, were formally committed.

But the example of Massachusetts brought matters in the New Hampshire grants to a crisis. The people, sympathizing with their New England friends and kindred, felt painfully their forced connection with New York, a province with whom they now seemed to have less sympathy than ever. The regular term of the court for the county of Cumberland, was to have been holden in March, 1775. Efforts were made to dissuade the judges from holding the court. Of course, while they held their commission, they would not consent to identify themselves with the rebellious party. They proceeded in their official course, and the inhabitants of Westminster and the adjacent towns, followed the Massachusetts precedent, and took possession of the court house. The judges did not, however, follow the wise example of their brethren in the Bay State, who prudently withdrew before the pressure of the people. The judges appeared before the house attended with an armed posse, and commanded the crowd to disperse. Nothing more serious than hard words passed at this time, and the judges, sheriffs, and posse withdrew.

Negotiations now took place between the leaders of the people and the judges. A quasi armistice was agreed to, by which the people were to keep possession of the court house until morning. At that time the judges would come without their armed posse, and be admitted, to hear what the resistants might offer in defence of their course. Contrary to this understanding, after lulling the vigilance of the people, the sheriff and his followers came to the court house at midnight and demanded admittance. Being refused, they fired into the building, and by this treacherous act killed one man, and wounded several more. The wounded men, and some others who were seized amid the terror and confusion, they committed to prison. It was well for the attacking party that this outrage was not committed on the western side of the mountains, in the province proper of the Green Mountain Boys.

The news of this outrage flew apace. At an early hour the next day a crowd had collected. A coroner's jury was impanelled; a verdict of murder was returned against the officers, several of whom were arrested. Notwithstanding the exasperation of the multitude, it does not appear that any violence was done to the prisoners, who were conveyed to the jail in Northampton, in the province of Massachusetts. Upon application of the chief justice of New York, they were released, and returned home. Massachusetts could claim no jurisdiction in the case, and their committal to a prison in that province was manifestly illegal; though to seek their punishment in the jurisdiction of New York would have been fruitless. Now the settlers east of the mountains made common cause with their brethren. A meeting was convened in Westminster, on the 11th of April, at which was passed the following resolve: "that it is the duty of the inhabitants wholly to renounce and resist the government of New York, until such time as the lives and property of the inhabitants may be secured by it; or until such time as they can have opportunity to lay their grievances before his most gracious majesty in council, with a proper remonstrance against the unjustifiable conduct of that government, together with a humble petition to be taken out of so oppressive a jurisdiction, and either annexed to some other government, or erected and incorporated into a new one, as may appear best for the inhabitants."

While the people of the New Hampshire grants were in this state of excitement, events occurred which gave their thoughts a new direction, or rather which gave them, in the same direction, a higher object; and which led their spirit of resistance beyond New York, to contend with the power from whom the authorities assumed to derive their right to oppress. On the 19th of April, 1775, occurred the battle of Lexington; and while some of the higher spirited men in Vermont were taking measures for armed resistance against the authorities of New York, the news of this first blood shed in the contest with Great Britain reached the excited settlers. "By presenting new scenes, and greater objects," says Dr. Williams, the historian of Vermont, "this event seems to have prevented either party from proceeding to hostilities; and turned their attention from their particular contest to the general cause of America. The attention of all orders of men was immediately engaged; local and provincial contests were at once swallowed up by the novelty, the grandeur, and the importance of the contest that opened between Britain and America."

At this date, 1775, the population of Vermont is estimated by Mr. Thompson, author of the Gazetteer of Vermont, at 20,000. The population had grown up by immigration in fifteen years; for in 1760, there were not more than three hundred people in the territory. These settlers were fully qualified for the service they were afterward to perform. Schooled amid privations and difficulties, they were trained to perform the important part which they subsequently supported in the war of the Revolution.

CHAPTER V.

Benedict Arnold — The surprise of Crown Point and Ticonderoga recommended — Arnold commissioned and authorized to attempt it — A detachment of volunteers organized in Connecticut for the same purpose — Form a junction with Ethan Allen and a party of Green Mountain Boys — Meeting with Arnold — Appointed second in command — Disputes between Arnold and Allen — Capture of Ticonderoga — Of Crown Point — Of Skeensboro — St. John's surprised by Arnold — Approach of the British — Congress provides for the restitution of the captured property — Massachusetts and the continental congress — Surrender of authority to the latter — George Washington appointed commander-in-chief of the colonial forces — Powers assumed by congress — Petitions and addresses to Great Britain — Judicious conduct of the English parliament in respect to Canada — Ticonderoga and Crown Point efficiently garrisoned.

THE courage and patriotism of the Green Mountain Boys were now offered a wider field than that in which they had hitherto been exercised. The struggle with Great Britain had commenced in earnest; and as General Gage had taken the initiatory steps of hostility, by the seizure of warlike stores, the colonists thought it a proper retaliation to possess themselves of the posts and munitions belonging to and occupied by the crown. The importance of the fortifications on the Champlain route from New York to Canada, suggested movements in Connecticut and Massachusetts, with a view to their reduction; and although these movements were simultaneously made, they were undertaken without concert. Benedict Arnold, who, in the early part of the Revolutionary war, distinguished himself as an able and courageous officer, called the attention of the Massachusetts committee of safety to the fortresses of Crown Point and Ticonderoga. Arnold belonged by birth and residence to Connecticut, and was thus aware of the quantity of munitions at these points, and of the state of the defences. He had been a dealer in horses, and subsequently a trader and shipmaster in New Haven. He repaired to Boston on the breaking out of hostilities, in command of a company of volunteers; and upon his representations of the state of Ticonderoga and Crown Point, he received a colonel's commission, with authority to raise a regiment in Vermont for the enterprise.

Meanwhile, certain gentlemen in Connecticut set the same plan on foot. They knew that the garrisons were then feeble at both points, and the fortifications dilapidated, and hastened to secure the two places before they should be put in a better posture of defence. A loan of eighteen hundred dollars was obtained of the legislature, powder and ball were procured, and the Connecticut party, of forty men, set forward to communicate with Ethan Allen. Seth Warner, who had figured in the Green Mountain proceedings with Ethan Allen, readily acted with his old chief in this new enterprise. The affair altogether appears to have been conducted with great address and promptitude. The attacking party was advised of all the turns and passages of the works at Ticonderoga, by Captain Noah Phelps, one of the Connecticut volunteers, who introduced himself into the fort, and professing great clownishness and simplicity, examined the place with the eye of a veteran.

Arnold had, meanwhile, joined Allen at Castleton. He came attended only by a servant, having failed to obtain recruits, since Allen and Warner, men known to the settlers, had been before him. Arnold would have assumed the command, but to this the Green Mountain Boys would not submit. A council was called, and Arnold's commission was examined. He was permitted to join as a volunteer, but Allen was also elected and commissioned colonel, and Arnold was recognised under his Massachusetts commission as second in command.

On the evening of the 9th of May, Colonel Allen arrived at Orwell, with two hundred and seventy men, all except forty of whom were Green Mountain Boys. Some difficulty was found in procuring boats, but the people of the vicinity fell readily into the spirit of the enterprise. Two young men, who overheard in bed what was going forward, corrupted the boatmen of Major Skeen with that potent ammunition, a bottle of rum, and inveigled the unconscious men into the service, boat and all. They discovered their mistake when, at Shoreham, the point of embarkation on the Vermont side, they were put under guard as prisoners of war. Other boats were also procured, but all were only of sufficient capacity to transport eighty men at one trip. Here again the dispute for precedence between the two colonels was renewed. Arnold demanded the honour of leading the men into the fort. Allen refused to suffer it; and the dispute was settled by a compromise that both should enter together, but that Allen should enter on the right, and have the command.

Just before daybreak on the 10th of May the first party of eighty-three men landed on the shore near Ticonderoga. The hour requiring expedition, if a surprise was to be attempted, Allen decided to proceed at once, without waiting for the residue of his men. He made a short harangue to his party, which he concluded by saying: "I now propose to advance before you, and conduct you in person through the wicket gate; but inasmuch as it is a desperate attempt, I do not urge it on any one contrary to his will. You that will undertake it voluntarily, poise your firelocks." Not a man hesitated.

With celerity and in perfect silence they moved to the attack, Colonel Allen at the head. The sentry at the gate snapped his fusee, but it missed fire, and the party followed him up as he retreated through the covered way. The other sentries were seized; and except these not a soul was awake in the fort, until the cheers of the Green Mountain Boys, drawn up in line on the parade, startled the garrison in astonishment from their slumbers. The idea of an enemy had not entered into their dreams, and the thought of surprise and capture was the last that could have occurred to them. Captain de Laplace, the commander, was confronted by Colonel Allen in his quarters, before he had time to dress, with a demand for the surrender of the fort. "By what authority?" asked the amazed officer. "I demand it," said Colonel Allen, "in the name of the Continental Congress," adding one of the irreverent expressions to which the colonel of the Green Mountain Boys was too much addicted. Captain de Laplace had no choice but to submit. It was a complete surprise in every sense; for while the captain surrendered, he did not know under what authority his captor was acting. The news of the Lexington affair had not yet reached Ticonderoga.

On the same day Colonel Seth Warner took possession of Crown Point, with as little difficulty as Ticonderoga had been captured. Skeensboro, now called Whitehall, was also taken by another party. Thus while Major Skeen was absent in England, ended his well-meant efforts to govern a new province, to be erected out of the disputed New Hampshire grants.

The total garrisons of these places did not amount to more than seventy men. But the stores and ammunition which fell into the hands of the captors, were the best results of the day's work. Over two hundred pieces of artillery, a large supply of powder, provisions, and materials for boat building, were among the property secured, and all without the loss of a man, or the infliction of a wound upon either party. A schooner seized at Skeensboro played also a useful part in the subsequent proceedings. The party who had captured it joined Arnold, and with these men he put in use his nautical experience; and assumed upon the water the precedence which Allen had refused him upon the land. A number of batteaux were procured, of which Allen took command. The wind giving the schooner the advantage, she outsailed the batteaux, and reaching St. John's, Arnold there surprised and captured a British armed vessel, the only one then on the lake, and returned with his prize to Ticonderoga. In this expedition a large addition was made to the valuable munitions of war which were seized by the Americans. Colonel Allen proposed to take and hold St. John's, but was obliged to retire by the appearance of a superior force, which entered the place from Montreal. As the result of the six days' work, Lake Champlain and its fortresses fell into the hands of the Americans; the main actors in these important successes being the proscribed Green Mountain Boys. So little, however, did the continental congress anticipate the result of the war thus commenced, that an inventory of the property captured was ordered to be taken, that at the close of the difficulty restitution of it might be made to the British government. The same congress, however, made such provision for the public service, that it was evident they considered the difficulty one which must be resolutely met.

A full detail of the recent events in Massachusetts, the measures of Gage, the affairs of Lexington and Concord, and the oppressive acts of the British parliament, were laid before congress. Massachusetts led the way in giving the congress a legislative and executive power which the former congress had not assumed. The Massachusetts provincial congress asked advice as to the form of government to be assumed, now that the British government had violated the charter of the province; and they, likewise, desired the continental congress to assume command of the troops assembled before Boston.

In answer to these appeals, the continental congress recommended that Massachusetts should still act under her charter as near as might be under the circumstances. The governor appointed by the king, in conformity with the charter, they could not recognise, since he had set the charter aside. The councillors appointed by the king they would not recognise, since these appointments were a violation of the charter. According to the suggestion of congress they elected representatives, those representatives chose counsellors, and the counsellors exercised the powers formerly vested in the governor and council. In relation to the other request that the continental congress would assume the charge of the army, congress resolved that hostilities had been commenced by Great Britain, and that, therefore, the colonies ought to be put in a state of defence; that no provisions should be furnished to the British army or navy; that no bills drawn by British officers ought to be negotiated; and that colonial ships ought not to be employed in the transportation of British troops. And while congress denied any intention to throw off their allegiance, the appointment of George Washington commander-in-chief, was unanimously made, and other officers were commissioned, thus creating a complete military establishment so far as the provision of officers were considered.

Thus did congress, in part, assume supreme power, and in part accept investment with it. Without precedents to refer to, and with no guides but patriotism, discretion, and a spirit of conciliation, this patriotic body undertook and maintained a work to which no other revolutionary tribunal was ever competent. Much was done by tacit agreement. They formed their own precedents, were determined in their progress by their own past usage, and met new exigencies with a wisdom to which the history of the world affords no parallel. Continental appointments and commissions superseded or controlled provincial appointments; and although there were unquestionably some heart-burnings, jealousies, and complaints, yet each submitted for the good of the whole, and the petition of Massachusetts put congress in command of the army through all the colonies, and for the whole period of the war. And if the continental congress was not, as in the course of our narrative will be shown, of power sufficient to compel justice in all cases where their power was invoked so to do, we may wonder that such a body could accomplish so much, rather than be surprised that there were some things to which it was not equal.

As we are not writing the history of the war, but only of one state in this confederacy, the general narrative will need to be introduced only so far as it is necessary to the history of Vermont. Among the leading acts of the congress which assembled in the spring of 1775, besides those which we have already noticed, were the compilation of "Articles of War;" the provision of means for prosecuting it; and the setting forth of a "Declaration of the Causes and Necessity of taking up Arms." A petition to the king was adopted, and an address to the inhabitants of Great Britain. A letter of thanks to the mayor and livery of London for their spirited opposition to the ministerial oppression of the colonies was prepared. Addresses were also published to the people of Ireland, of Jamaica, and of the Canadas. Indian boards were appointed to treat with and conciliate the aborigines; and a post-office system was organized, at the head of which was placed Dr. Franklin, just displaced from the royal mail establishment.

Some of the addresses above mentioned were repetitions of those issued by a former congress. Almost the only politic movement adopted by the British parliament, in the controversy with the provinces, had been taken in relation to Canada. By the act called the Quebec Act, the old French law was restored in that province, and the Roman church was guaranteed the possession of its immense property. The boundaries of the province were extended so as to include that part of the territory now belonging to the United States, which lies north of the Ohio River, and west of the Mississippi. This act, unpalatable to the small number of Englishmen in the conquered province, and obnoxious to the other colonies, was more potent than an army in securing Canada to Great Britain. It secured the support of the clergy and the seigneurs; and whatever temporary success attended American invasions, prevented that province, through their influence, from joining the American confederacy. The chances of war offered the Canadians their choice between allegiance to a king who had just conferred upon them unlooked for advantages, and association with a people who had been active personal enemies in the colonial wars, and who were as much disliked as protestants, as they were hated as national enemies. Therefore the addresses of the continental congress, and the efforts of the continental army, were alike ineffectual; and no small ground of this ill success was to be found in the fact, that while the Canadians were very affectionately appealed to in the addresses of congress, in other documents emanating from the same body they were alluded to in terms of disrespect.

The battle of Bunker Hill followed the skirmishes at Lexington and Concord, and the seizure of Ticonderoga and Crown Point. The war had now in reality begun past recall, and the organization of the army made available the possession of Lake Champlain and its posts. They were garrisoned by troops under the command of officers holding commissions in the continental army. The possession of such advantages of position led the way to a series of offensive operations against Canada, in which the Green Mountain Boys largely partook.

CHAPTER VI.

Colonel Allen — Volunteer officers — Their difficulties with respect to rank in the continental army — Arnold superseded in command at Ticonderoga — Returns to Massachusetts — Attempt upon Canada — Defenceless condition of that province — Regiment of Green Mountain Boys raised by Colonel Warner — Schuyler and Montgomery appointed to command the invading army — Supineness of the Canadians — Activity of General Carleton — Advance of Schuyler and Montgomery — Abortive attempt on Montreal — Ethan Allen captured and sent to England — Incidents of his captivity — Taking of Chambly by the Americans — Repulse of Carleton at Longue-isle by Colonel Warner — Surrender of St John's to Montgomery — Surrender of Montreal — Narrow escape of Carleton — March of Arnold through the wilderness to Quebec — He forms a junction with Montgomery — Attempt on Quebec and death of Montgomery — Gallantry and hardihood of Arnold.

UPON the capture of Ticonderoga and the other Champlain stations, Colonel Allen appears to have returned home, leaving Arnold in charge, that officer having a regular commission under the authority of Massachusetts. There was no provincial government in Vermont to grant commissions, and Allen must have held his post as a volunteer, his rank being determined by the men under his command. Much difficulty, we may here observe, occurred in the early organization of the continental army, from the claims of volunteer officers to rank according to the number of men they were able to bring with them; and though this served the purpose of raising a large impromptu army, and collecting soldiers ready for an enthusiastic onslaught, it did not provide men patient of discipline, or disposed to that perfect subordination and calm endurance of camp privations which are necessary in all true soldiers. Allen was rather what, in later times, has been termed a guerilla chief than a regular officer.

Connecticut undertook to garrison these posts, and New York to supply them with provisions. Under this arrangement Arnold was superseded in the command at Ticonderoga, and being of a factious and troublesome spirit, ambitious and impatient of subordination, he disbanded his men, and returned to the camp before Boston. He was a disappointed man. He had written to congress, in conjunction with Allen, strongly urging a descent upon Canada; and he wished for the opportunity to distinguish himself in that expedition, the success of which he boldly predicted, as there were only two regiments of British regulars there. The greater part of the British forces on this continent were employed in the colonies which were actually in a state of insurrection; and the British government counted, not entirely without foundation, as events proved, upon the effects of the Quebec Bill, already mentioned. If this bill did not produce enthusiasm in favour of Britain—if, indeed, it changed discontent from one class to another in Canada, it still produced the effect desired upon the great body of the people, securing, with some exceptions, their indifference, if not their active co-operation with the British forces.

When first addressed upon the subject of invading Canada, congress was indisposed to enter upon offensive measures, preferring and vainly hoping to retain an attitude purely defensive. New York was particularly adverse at first to Arnold's project, but had voted to raise four regiments for the defence of the colony. To these four regiments was added another from the New Hampshire grants; and Colonel Seth Warner was commissioned under the authority of the continental congress to command this regiment of Green Mountain Boys. Five thousand men were voted for the northern service, including the regiments above named, and the Connecticut regiments in garrison on Lake Champlain. The command of this force was given to Major-Generals Philip Schuyler and Richard Montgomery.

Rumours prevailed that the British government was making exertions to induce the Canadians and Indians to fall upon the frontier of the colonies. It was, therefore, decided to invade the province; and it was proposed to detail two thousand men for that purpose. These men united with their warlike mission a sort of political propagandism. They were to treat the Canadians as friends and brothers, and were plentifully provided with such ammunition as proclamations and circular letters, exhorting the Canadians to arouse and assert their liberties, and declaring that the Americans entered their country not as enemies, but as friends and protectors. Gen. Schuyler was authorized, "should he find the measure *not disagreeable to the Canadians*," to take possession of St. John's and Montreal.

33

General Carleton, the governor of Canada, was a man possessed of great energy and address, or he would not have been able to save the province to his royal master. Expectation in England was very much disappointed in relation to the conduct of the Canadians. Twenty thousand stand of arms, and other military stores were sent out to Canada, to equip the inhabitants, who, it was supposed, would readily enlist; and in lieu of transporting troops from Europe, the Canadians were to be used to overwhelm their rebellious neighbours. But the Canadians absolutely refused to march out of the province. They would defend it, if attacked, but not embark in a quarrel which they did not understand. The Bishop of Quebec was appealed to, but very properly refused to aid General Carleton by an episcopal mandate. The clergy issued letters, and the seigneurs interested themselves, but the principal effect which these conflicting appeals from both sides, American and British, produced, was to make the great body of the people remain neutral, although some of them enlisted in both armies. The American proclamations, however, secured the invaders from molestation from the Canadians, except when the latter were compelled by the presence of British regulars to take part in the contest.

The provision of materials for boat building, found at Ticonderoga, at the time of its capture by the Americans in the spring, now came into service. While preparations were maturing for the invasion, intelligence was received that General Carleton, with characteristic energy, was pushing forward to check it; and fearing that he would get possession of the lake, and thus turn their projected invasion into a defence of their own territory, Generals Schuyler and Montgomery, in August, proceeded down the lake to Isle Aux Noix, an islet in the Sorel River, commanding its navigation, and there prepared to defend the passage. From thence they circulated letters and proclamations through the adjacent country; and on the 6th of September were permitted to advance without molestation toward St. John's. This is a town at the head of the navigation of the river, and an important point. A landing was effected, the place was reconnoitered, and after a skirmish with an Indian party in which the savages were repulsed, the Americans fell back to the Isle Aux Noix. They found St. John's too well garrisoned and defended to be assaulted without artillery.

General Schuyler went back to Albany to hasten forward supplies, and left Montgomery in charge. On the 17th, having received reinforcements, General

Montgomery pushed forward for a second attempt on St. John's. The place was garrisoned by nearly all the regular troops in the province, some six or eight hundred men, and was well supplied with artillery and the munitions of war. The first duty of Montgomery was to gain over the inhabitants of the country, and to detach the Indians who had joined General Carleton. He wished to secure himself from being compelled to raise the siege by enemies without the town; and in this undertaking he appears fully to have succeeded. Parties of his troops were scattered over the country, and were favourably received by the Canadians. The settlers were, it may well be supposed, very willing to enter into a compromise which left the invasion entirely an affair between their British masters and the invaders, while their own property was secure from molestation or injury.

Colonel Allen, who of course accompanied the expedition, had command of one of these reconnoitering parties of eighty men. A portion of these were Green Mountain Boys—the residue Canadians. As Allen had commenced the successes of the American arms by the seizure of Ticonderoga and Crown Point, he was easily persuaded that Montreal, at that time the headquarters of General Carleton, might be added to his list of captures. A night attack was concerted between Allen and Major Brown. The latter, with two hundred men, was to land in the night, on the south side of Montreal, and Allen on the north, and both were to attack the post together. Allen landed with a little band of about one hundred men, but waited in vain for his ally, who failed to make his appearance. When daylight had made the surprise of the place impracticable even had Allen been in force, he might still have saved himself by a retreat, but rashly determined to maintain his position. He was overpowered by a superior force; and after a desperate resistance, in which fifteen of his men were killed, and several wounded, he was taken prisoner together with thirty-eight of his followers. General Carleton refused to recognise these captives as prisoners of war. They were loaded with irons as felons, and sent to England for trial. Such was the issue of a rash attempt, made by Allen without orders. General Carleton based his treatment on the plea that Allen was not a commissioned officer, but a leader of banditti.

At a subsequent period in our history, the name of this brave but erratic man will again appear in connection with the history of the state; and we may here give his private history until that reappearance. Allen published a

35

narrative of the events of his captivity, written in his usual strange style, but bearing the appearance of truthfulness. He was confined with his companions in a small apartment, on board of the vessel, with hand-cuffs upon their wrists. Perhaps the idea which he gave of his prowess at the time of his capture, may have contributed to this harsh treatment. If the intention of trying Allen as a felon was entertained by his captors, it was abandoned. After a month's imprisonment in Pendennis Castle, near Falmouth, he was sent back to America. For five months he was kept at Halifax, and thence transferred to New York. On the passage a plan was projected among the prisoners, of whom there were many, to kill the English captain, and seize the frigate in which they were transported. But as that officer treated Allen with great kindness, he refused to join the conspiracy, and his refusal defeated the plan. Allen was a prisoner in New York a year and a half, sometimes confined, and sometimes at large on parole. In May, 1778, he was exchanged, and, repairing to the headquarters of General Washington, was there treated with great respect. His health being shattered, he returned to Vermont to recruit, having made an offer of his services to the commander-in-chief when his health should be restored. He was received in Vermont by his old companions with great rejoicings; and as a mark of respect and confidence was appointed commander-in-chief of the militia of the state, but never had occasion to act in a military capacity. He resumed his pen, and besides the narrative of his captivity, published a "Vindication of the opposition of the inhabitants of Vermont to the government of New York, and of their right to form an independent state."

To return to our narrative. General Schuyler was prevented by sickness from accompanying the invading forces, and the command devolved upon General Montgomery. The force, by the arrival of reinforcements and the addition of Canadian volunteers, was now swelled to between two and three thousand men, but they were woefully deficient in military stores. Understanding that the little fortress of Chambly contained a large quantity of the munitions of war, Montgomery detailed a force against it, under Majors Brown and Livingston. The place was carried, after a short resistance, on the 18th of October, and the garrison, about one hundred men, surrendered prisoners of war. The standard of the 7th Regiment was taken, and immediately forwarded to congress, the first trophy which they received.

But what was much more valuable to the besiegers, was one hundred and twenty barrels of gunpowder, and a large quantity of military stores and provisions.

With this seasonable supply, Montgomery renewed the siege of St. John's with increased vigour. The garrison, momently expecting that the siege would be relieved by General Carleton, defended the post with courage and resolution. Carleton made great exertions to raise a force for the purpose, but the determination of the Canadians to keep as far as possible out of the contest, made the raising of a proper force exceedingly difficult. He was able to muster only one thousand men, including a few regulars, the militia of Montreal, Canadians and Indians. Another body of troops under the veteran officer, Colonel McLean, was posted at the junction of the Sorel with the St. Lawrence. These troops were the remains of a Highland brigade, which had settled in Canada, and with some other Scotch emigrants were re-mustered into the service.

It was of the last importance to General Carleton to effect a junction with Col. McLean. For this purpose he attempted to land at Longue-isle, opposite Montreal. But Colonel Seth Warner, with his Green Mountain regiment, who had detected and watched the movement, opened suddenly upon them such a well-directed and incessant fire of musketry, and grape from a single cannon, that the enemy was thrown into the greatest confusion, and soon driven into a disorderly retreat. As General Carleton's command was largely composed of Canadians, it was impossible to rally them, or lead them against the disadvantages of position, which only veterans would have overcome. The rout was complete. When the news of this reverse reached McLean, at his position at the junction of the Sorel, he saw the inutility of holding that post. His Canadian allies deserted him to a man. Having heard also that Quebec was threatened, he retreated with his Highlanders to that important point. Colonel Warner immediately took possession of the post which McLean had abandoned, and proceeded to erect batteries, to arm rafts, and take other measures which effectually commanded the River St. Lawrence, and shut off the vessels at Montreal from escaping down the river.

General Montgomery, upon receiving the gratifying intelligence of the defeat of General Carleton by Colonel Warner, at once advised the commander of the garrison at St. John's of the fact, and summoned him to surrender. As all hope of relief was now gone, and to contend further would have been madness, the garrison, on the 3d of November capitulated, being allowed the honours of war. They were treated with the greatest courtesy by General Montgomery. The regulars, five hundred in number, were sent by the way of Ticonderoga, into the interior of New England. The English commander had endeavoured to obtain, in his capitulation, permission for the garrison to go to England, but this General Montgomery positively refused; although the manner in which he dictated his terms to the vanquished, elicited this strong praise from an English contemporary historian: "In all transactions with our forces, Montgomery wrote, spoke, and behaved with that attention, regard, and politeness to both private men and officers, which might be expected from a man of worth and honour, who found himself involved in an unhappy quarrel with his friends and countrymen." As an illustration of the expectations of an early accommodation, still entertained, we may remark that while the officers were permitted to retain their swords, their other arms, it was promised, should be restored to them when the difficulty between the parent country and the colonies should pass away.

General Montgomery followed up his advantage by presenting himself before Montreal. General Carleton with his regulars retreated to the flotilla, and Montreal surrendered to Montgomery, who occupied the place with his troops. Vigorous preparations were now made to attack the vessels of Carleton, but that officer made his escape in a boat with muffled oars, during a dark night, and hastened to Quebec. The vessels, with their stores and munitions, were captured by the Americans; and the residue of the British force, in an attempt to escape, were also captured. Had Carleton himself but been among the prisoners, the Canadian invasion would have ended in a complete triumph.

Montgomery now pushed on for Quebec. But his force was reduced by the discharge of men whose term of enlistment had expired, and by the necessity of leaving garrisons at the forts he had captured, in order to keep open the communication with Lake Champlain. Only three hundred men followed him on his expedition against the capital of Canada. The winter march had its terrors, for it was near the close of November before it commenced. However, the woollens and other commissariat stores found in Montreal, in part abated the rigors of the service.

While the events which we have enumerated took place along the St. Lawrence, one of the most arduous military feats of the Revolutionary war was going on in another quarter. To take advantage of the absence of the Canadian force from Quebec, an expedition was planned to reach that city, by a march through the forests of Maine, and either reduce it in the deficiency of its defenders, or compel General Carleton to withdraw troops from Montreal for the defence of Quebec, and thus insure success to the American attempt on Montreal. After a march attended with almost incredible hardships, Arnold appeared before Quebec on the 9th of November. The march had occupied about six weeks; and from the time of leaving the last settlement on the Kennebec, to which point they were transported with comparative ease, the remainder of their route lay through an uninhabited wilderness. The command originally consisted of about a thousand men; but one-third, composing the rear division, turned back on account of the scarcity of provisions, and with the rest Arnold gallantly persevered. He had no other guide than the journal of a British officer, who had made the same journey some years before. But he was supported by the gallantry of his troops, who displayed a courage and fortitude in suffering never exceeded in the annals of warfare. When at length they reached the scattered habitations of the Canadians, their last morsel of food was consumed.

Bare time was taken to refresh the men and re-organize the troops, over whom there had been little attempt at discipline for the last few days of famishing. Proclamations of a similar tenor to those distributed among the Canadians by Montgomery were circulated. An Indian scout had been despatched to inform Generals Schuyler and Montgomery of the arrival of Arnold in Canada. Unfortunately, the scout fell into the hands of Colonel McLean, and that officer, as before related, hastened from Sorel to Quebec, with his Highlanders. When Arnold arrived at Point Leon, opposite Quebec, the high winds and want of boats rendered the passage of the river impossible. On the night of the 14th of November, he effected the transportation of his troops across—a wonderful feat, when we consider the frail nature of his boats, the danger of the rapid current, and the presence of the armed vessels. The very temerity of the undertaking caused its success.

On landing on the Quebec side, he had still nearly two miles march before he could find a place where the rugged cliffs could be surmounted. But he marched down the shore to Wolfe's cove, and with his hardy band, encountering the same obstacles that the British hero had surmounted, he stood at midnight, with the advance party, on the Heights of Abraham. He wished to press forward at once and attempt a surprise, but was overruled by his officers in a council of war. The opportunity of a surprise was lost, and Arnold had no artillery or other implements required for an assault. Nearly one-third of his muskets had been rendered useless by the hardships of the march through the wilderness, and of powder there was not more than sufficient for six or seven rounds to a man. Still he flattered himself that some defection in the town would yet put it into his hands. He paraded on the heights for some days, and sent two flags demanding a surrender. But General McLean, who had experience of American operations, and who probably feared what Arnold hoped, refused to suffer any communication with him, and even fired upon the flags as they approached. Fear united the disaffected; and while Arnold could hold no intercourse with the town, and thus failed in opportunity, and perhaps in inclination, to assure the people of the safety of their property, the heterogeneous population joined for defence; the sailors were landed to strengthen the garrison, and its force soon exceeded that of the besiegers. Under these discouraging circumstances Arnold retired to Point Aux Trembles, to await the arrival of General Montgomery. On his march he unconsciously passed General Carleton, who was on his way to Quebec.

Montgomery joined Arnold at the beginning of December, and comforted his half-naked troops with clothing and other necessaries. The united forces of the two expeditions did not exceed a thousand men, of whom only eight hundred could be counted effective. It was truly a forlorn and most desperate condition. The winter was too severe to attempt a regular siege, and the opening of spring would certainly bring reinforcements to the enemy. Under all these circumstances, and knowing the high expectations which were entertained in the colonies. General Montgomery at once determined on an assault.

Accordingly, on the night of the 31st of December it was attempted. Four parties approached the walls in four directions, and the plan was so well concerted that every part seemed equally threatened. A violent storm of snow made the attack less expected. Some Canadians, posted at a block-house, fled before Montgomery, throwing away their arms. He was himself at the head of his detachment, and the difficulties of the way had lengthened his line so much that he was compelled to wait until his men came up. He assisted with his own hands to remove obstructions. Meanwhile, the terror which the fugitives had occasioned within the walls somewhat abated; and as Montgomery rapidly advanced at the head of his men, one or two of the garrison had ventured to return to the battery which commanded the pass. One of them seized a match and discharged a gun. This accidental fire proved fatal to the enterprise and its commander. Montgomery fell, and with him Captains McPherson and Cheeseman, an orderly sergeant and a private, all the result of a chance fire. The party, dispirited, instantly retreated, and the whole strength of the garrison was turned to the repulse of Arnold. Of the four apparent attacks two were feints, those only commanded by Arnold and Montgomery being real. Arnold was thrown out of the combat by a ball which shattered his leg, and he was carried off the field. Captain Daniel Morgan then led the attack, but succeeded only in forcing his way into a place from which, after a bloody contest, his retreat was cut off. He was compelled, with three hundred and forty men, to surrender; and the loss in killed, principally in Arnold's division, was over sixty.

We have pursued this account of the invasion of Canada with the more minuteness, since its way lay through Vermont; and the seizure of the posts on Lake Champlain, by which the enterprise was suggested, was the work of the Green Mountain Boys. They aided largely in the successful operations on the Sorel River. And they, too, were active in the events which followed the disastrous retreat, which was at last compensated for by the capture of Burgoyne. To the history of Vermont, more than to that of any other of the states, does this passage in our annals belong.

By the abortive attempt on Canada, the fact was demonstrated that a union, by the free will of the Canadians, to the other colonies was not to be counted upon. They would cheerfully, perhaps, have acquiesced could the other provinces have expelled the British from them; but they seemed willing to incur neither loss, exposure, nor expense for the advancement of either party. And when they perceived that the continental congress, instead of sending an army into Canada to hold it against the British, and to enrich the province by the purchase of supplies, relied upon the efforts of the Canadians themselves, they became very loyal subjects of Great Britain; particularly in the expectation of the arrival of British reinforcements.

Colonel Arnold fell back three miles from Quebec, and with wonderful perseverance and hardihood put on a complexion of confidence which retained the respect of the Canadians. The remains of his shattered force were kept together, and through the winter the blockade of Quebec was kept up. General Carleton attempted no sorties; and behind their ramparts of ice and snow, the gallant little besieging party awaited succour. Despatches had been sent to Montreal for assistance, and in the colonies efforts were immediately made to raise and forward reinforcements.

CHAPTER VII.

The people of the New Hampshire grants apply to congress for advice — Their anomalous position — Convention at Dorset and petition to congress — The memorial withdrawn — Resumption of operations in Canada — Difficulties of Arnold with the Canadians — Breaking out in camp of the small-pox — Arnold takes command at Montreal, and is succeeded by General Thomas before Quebec — Arrival of relief to Quebec — Retreat of the Americans to Sorel — Death of General Thomas — Unfortunate attempt to surprise Three Rivers — Retreat to St. John's — To Isle Aux Noix — To Ticonderoga — General Sullivan is superseded by General Gates — Organization of a naval force — Difficulties with which it was attended — British preparations — General Arnold appointed to command the American flotilla — Engagement on the 11th of October — Great superiority of the British force — Renewed engagement on the 13th — Gallant conduct of Arnold — Summary of results — Sir Guy Carleton menaces Ticonderoga, but returns to winter quarters without an attack.

CONGRESS now (1775-6) had representatives from the Thirteen United Colonies, Georgia having come into the confederation, and New York being convinced that temporizing measures would serve no longer. The Green Mountain Boys, although they had a regiment in the continental army, were as yet unassigned, and belonged to no government. In this difficulty, probably influenced by the example of Massachusetts, they sent deputies to Philadelphia to ask advice of congress as to what course it was best for them to pursue. But these gentlemen had not the advantage of membership of that body, and could only obtain informal and individual counsel. The opinion of several leading members was, that they should form a temporary association for the management of the business of the whole population on the New Hampshire grants, and conduct their local affairs by committees.

The people had already adopted these suggestions. Their government had been managed by meetings of towns, by committees, officers, and by leaders— sometimes appointed in public meetings, and sometimes acting by the implied consent of the public. This state of things, particularly west of the mountains, had grown out of the necessity for union to resist the aggressions of New York. But now that the need of association to resist the overt acts of that province had ceased, the people began to feel their anomalous position. They were willing to take part in the struggle against Great Britain, but they were not willing to be mustered into the service as belonging to the province or colony of New York; for such an admission would be a virtual surrender of all they had been contending for. And they desired something more positive than the unofficial recommendations of members of congress in their private capacity.

In order to procure some definite arrangement, the people of the New Hampshire grants met in convention at Dorset, on the 16th of January, 1776. They drew up a memorial, which they styled "The humble petition, address, and remonstrance of that part of America, being situated south of Canada line, west of Connecticut River, commonly called and known by the name of the New Hampshire grants." They avowed their readiness, in this memorial, to bear a full proportion for the support of the contest in which the colonies were engaged; they expressed their zeal in the common cause, and their willingness to be called upon whenever congress should judge it necessary. But they declared their reluctance to put themselves under the provincial government of New York, because they would do nothing which might afterward be construed into an acknowledgment of the authority of that province. And they concluded by requesting that whenever congress should find it necessary to call upon them, they should not be called upon as inhabitants of New York, or as persons subject to the limitations, restrictions, or regulations of the militia of that province, but as inhabitants of the New Hampshire grants. And they prayed that whatever commissions should be granted to any of their inhabitants, might be so worded as to respect their position in this particular.

The effect of action upon this petition, by congress, would have been to determine the points in dispute between the contending parties. It is true that an effort was made to pursue a middle course. The committee to whom the memorial was referred, reported a recommendation that the petitioners should submit for the present to the government of New York, and assist their countrymen in the contest with Great Britain; but that such submission ought not to prejudice their right to any land in controversy, or be construed to affirm or admit the jurisdiction of New York, when the troubles then existing should be ended. Mr. Heman Allen, the agent of Vermont, justly considered that this report, if adopted, and its resolution passed, would weaken the position of the petitioners, by putting them in an antagonistic position with congress if they refused to submit, as be judged they would; or would do prejudice to their cause with New York if they acceded, the promise to the contrary notwithstanding. Under such circumstances, Mr. Allen deemed it prudent to withdraw the petition, and he obtained leave so to do. The petition was withdrawn on the 4th of June. One month later congress published the Declaration of Independence.

With the opening of spring, Arnold resumed active operations against Quebec, as far as his circumstances would admit. Reinforcements were under orders from the United Colonies, but the nature of the route they were obliged to take, and the severity of the Canadian winter, impeded their advance, and on the 1st day of May, 1776, the American force before Quebec did not exceed nineteen hundred men. The position of the army in reference to the Canadians had become most unfortunate. While Washington declared, in a letter to General Schuyler, that "Canada could only be secured by laying hold of the affections of the people, and engaging them heartily in the common cause;" and while congress fully endorsed this opinion by their acts and resolutions, circumstances entirely frustrated this enlightened policy. After the death of Montgomery, who had all the suavity of the gentleman united to the courage of the soldier, the efforts to conciliate the people, which had formed a part of the plan of the invasion, were interrupted. The priests were neglected, and their wavering course now terminated in adhesion to the cause of the crown. A commission, consisting of Dr. Franklin, Samuel Chase, and Charles Carroll, of Carrollton, was sent by congress into Canada with full powers to treat with the provincials. But the mission was too late, and did not reach Montreal until the tide had so completely turned that the invasion was abandoned as hopeless.

Congress had resolved that those Canadians who adhered to the American cause should be compensated for any injury that they might suffer. But this resolution weighed little against the stubborn facts and necessities of the case. To supply the wants of the army, General Arnold issued a proclamation making paper money current, and promising to redeem it in four months, and declaring those enemies who should refuse to receive it. Military orders proved no better than civil edicts in giving value to a valueless currency, and great discontents were caused among the Canadians by the effort at coercion. General Carleton made good use of the dissatisfaction of the Canadians, and was not without hope of raising the siege of Quebec through their assistance. Early in the spring he detached sixty men from the garrison, to form the nucleus of a relieving force. The Canadians were joining it in great numbers when Arnold sent a detachment, which routed the party. Arnold had despatched an express to Wooster, who was at Montreal, to bring succours and assume the command. Wooster arrived on the 1st of April, and on the next day Arnold received an injury by the fall of his horse, which confined him for some time to his bed.

To add to the discomfort and peril of the small American force, the small-pox now broke out among the troops. So great was the terror from this loathsome disease, that it was with difficulty the army could be saved from total dispersion. Discipline and order were out of the question; and the ineffectiveness of the besieging force was increased by the fact that the soldiers, in defiance of orders to the contrary, inoculated themselves, as that course was understood to diminish the danger of the disease. General Arnold retired to Montreal and took command of that post.

General Thomas, who had been appointed by congress to the command of the Canadian army, arrived at the camp near Quebec on the first of May. He found the small force so enfeebled by sickness, that not more than nine hundred men were effective, and of these three hundred were entitled to their discharge, and clamorously demanded it. Some show of operations had been made against Quebec; but under the disadvantage of want of men and munitions nothing was accomplished. Early in May, the British ship Isis—name ominous of hope to the royalists—forced her way up to Quebec with men and supplies. General Thomas, before this arrival, had determined upon falling back, and teams and men were promised by the inhabitants to assist in the removal of stores. But the fickle Canadians went over to the royalists, and the American army not only lost their aid but all means of an orderly retreat. The British re-captured the vessels which the Americans had taken. On the sixth of May, the very day of the landing of the reinforcements, General Carleton marched out at noon, with eight hundred men, to give battle to the Americans in their camp. He found it deserted by all who were in a condition to travel; and so precipitate had the movement been, that most of the sick and all the military stores fell into his hands. The sick, not only in camp, but such as were in huts and concealed in the woods, were sought out by proclamation, and treated with the most humane attention. The Americans continued their retreat till they reached the junction of the Sorel and the St. Lawrence, and there General Thomas was seized with the small-pox and died.

Large reinforcements had now arrived to the assistance of the British in Canada, making their number about thirteen thousand men. Their advanced post was at Three Rivers. The Americans at Sorel were joined by about four thousand men under General Sullivan, who reached that post early in June. Previous to his arrival, General Thompson, who had succeeded to the command upon the death of General Thomas, had despatched an expedition to surprise Three Rivers. It was understood that at that post there were only about eight hundred men, composing the advance of the British army. General Sullivan, upon assuming the command, sent General Thompson, with fourteen hundred men, to the aid of the detachment already sent to Three Rivers. The result was most disastrous. The Americans, who had counted on surprising the enemy, were delayed and discovered. They were repulsed in the attack on the village, and their retreat being cut off, two hundred men were made prisoners, including General Thompson and Colonel Irwin. About thirty Americans were killed, while the British loss was inconsiderable.

On the 14th of June, having with him only about two thousand five hundred effective men, General Sullivan was compelled to retreat from Sorel, and fell back to Chambly. Here he was joined by Arnold, who had been compelled to evacuate Montreal. That post had been menaced by a superior British force, its outposts having fallen into the hands of the enemy, who now, in full strength, and flushed with success, were driving the Americans rapidly before them. The Canadians and Indians, sure on which side the greatest strength lay, were no longer passive, but flocked to the royal standard. From Chambly, the remains of the American army, now so much inferior to the British that resistance was out of the question, fell back to St. John's. As the British under Carleton entered Chambly on one side, the Americans marched out on the other.

On the 18th of June, Sir Guy Carleton reached St. John's in the evening. The Americans had retreated, taking every thing of value. A detachment of the American army remained behind to complete the demolition of the fort and barracks, and left the place just as the enemy approached. The armed vessels on the Sorel and St. Lawrence Rivers were destroyed to prevent their falling into the hands of the British, but all the baggage of the army and nearly all the stores were saved. At Chambly there are falls in the river which precluded the possibility of saving the larger vessels. The batteaux were dragged up the rapids, and served for the embarkation of the troops. At St. John's the pursuit by the British ceased, as they had no flotilla which could be carried over the rapids. General Sullivan conducted the retreat with consummate skill and caution, and received the thanks of congress for his conduct; and General Carleton was rewarded for repelling the invasion by the Order of the Bath. It is seldom that the successful and unsuccessful both are complimented by their governments. The American army proceeded up Lake Champlain to Crown Point, and thence to Ticonderoga, where General Sullivan was succeeded in the command by General Gates, and measures were taken to restore the health and recruit the strength of men, who, in the strong language of John Adams, were "disgraced, defeated, discontented, dispirited, diseased, undisciplined, eaten up with vermin, no clothes, beds, blankets, or medicines, and no victuals but salt and flour." The temptation to alliteration must have prompted part of that sentence. Defeated the army certainly was, but it was by the rigors of the climate, and by a vastly superior force—defeated but not disgraced. It was an unfortunate expedition—undertaken under what proved to be a very wrong estimate of the character of the Canadians; but it gave opportunity for the exhibition of prodigies of valor, remarkable address, and wonderful endurance of hardship. The honour paid to Sir Guy Carleton by the British crown was no less a compliment to the American army than to the successful general.

Additional troops arrived at the head-quarters of General Gates, and the new recruits were assembled at Skeensboro, (now Whitehall,) to escape the danger of infection from the small-pox. A hospital was established for the sick, and by patient drilling the effects of the disasters of the late invasion were corrected in the older troops, while the new levies were schooled in military tactics. Another important matter also required attention. It was well understood that the pursuit of the American army beyond the Sorel was only prevented by the want of a naval armament on the part of the British; and that they were as fast as possible providing the necessary means of prosecuting the war. General Gates took command on the 12th of July. General Schuyler was appointed to the lake service, and by the 18th of August following had succeeded in refitting, building, and equipping fifteen vessels of different sizes. This work was done under great disadvantages, not the least of which was the difficulty of procuring shipwrights. The privateers and national vessels building at the different seaports, employed so many men, that it was almost impossible to induce the requisite workmen to go to Lake Champlain. But trees were felled in the woods and dragged by hand to the lake shore, and naval equipments were transported over roads almost impassable, with a vigour and resolution which marked the enterprises of that day, and which seemed to rise in proportion to the obstacles which were to be surmounted.

Meanwhile the British had obtained vessels constructed in England expressly for this service. Although it was found that the larger ones could not be got over the falls of the Sorel River at Chambly, this difficulty was surmounted by taking them in pieces, transporting them by land-carriage, and reconstructing them above the falls. There were about thirty vessels, ships, schooners, radeaux or rafts, and gun-boats, intended for attack and defence. There were also a sufficient number of boats for burden and the transportation of troops. These vessels were manned by eight hundred men, drafted from the British fleet, besides a detachment of artillerists to serve the guns. There were more seamen alone on board the British flotilla than the American complement of sailors and soldiers. The British force may be safely estimated at double that of the American. The metal of the British guns was heavier, and in all respects their vessels were better appointed.

General Arnold, of whose nautical experience we have before spoken, was put at the head of the American flotilla, and most of the vessels were commanded by officers of the army. Zeal and resolution, and the American faculty of adaptation to circumstances, stood them instead of skill and experience. On the 11th of October, the British flotilla offered battle to the American, and presented itself in full force, so confident of victory that it came into the engagement under the disadvantage of an unfavourable wind. The larger vessels could not be brought into action, but good service was done by the long boats of the British, which could creep to windward. The contest was kept up for several hours, the Americans maintaining their ground. No

49

vessel was captured on either side, though two of the British gondolas were destroyed, and an American schooner was burned and a gondola sunk. One or two vessels were much crippled, and sixty men, on the American side, were killed or wounded. The British acknowledged a loss of forty. The British drew off and anchored out of gun-shot, intending to renew the attack in the morning.

Finding that to contend with a force so superior was out of the question, General Arnold got under weigh in the night, and, favoured by the darkness and the fog, escaped with all his vessels. The British flotilla pursued, but the wind was adverse, and slow progress was made by either. On the 12th nothing occurred but the loss of one American gondola, which was overtaken and captured by the pursuers, and the abandonment of others, which were sunk to prevent their being captured. On the 13th, at noon, the British flotilla came within gunshot of the Americans. The Congress galley, on board of which was Arnold, and the Washington galley, General Waterbury, covered the retreat of the American flotilla. The Washington galley, having been disabled on the 11th, was compelled to strike. Arnold, in the Congress, defended himself "like a lion." The galley carried ten guns, and was at once engaged with the ship Inflexible of sixteen guns, the schooner Mann of fourteen, and the Carleton of twelve. He occupied these three vessels long enough to permit the escape of four or five of his flotilla, which made their way safe to Ticonderoga, the encounter taking place near Crown Point. It was now a struggle for trophies on the one hand, and for escape of men and destruction of vessels on the other. In spite of strenuous efforts of the British, Arnold managed to run his galley and some other vessels on shore, and blow them up after landing the men. The Congress blew up with colours flying, and the "bones" of the gallant little craft were to be seen upon the beach near Otter Creek for many years. The Americans lost eleven vessels and ninety men. The British had one vessel blown up and two sunk, and their loss in men was reported at fifty.

The character of the engagement is thus stated by Cooper in his Naval History of the United States. "Although the result of this action was so disastrous, the American arms gained much credit by their obstinate resistance. General Arnold, in particular, covered himself with glory, and his example appears to have been nobly followed by most of his officers and men. Even the enemy did justice to the resolution and skill with which the

American flotilla was managed, the disparity in the force rendering victory out of the question from the first. The manner in which the Congress was fought, until she had covered the retreat of the galleys, and the stubborn resolution with which she was defended until destroyed, converted the disasters of this part of the day into a species of triumph."

An attack on Ticonderoga was now apprehended. The fortress of Crown Point had been occupied by the Americans as an outpost, but General Gates withdrew the garrison, destroyed the fortifications, and every thing else which could not be removed. He concentrated his forces at Ticonderoga, and was soon joined by new levies, and with the restoration of the sick found himself at the head of twelve thousand effectives. Sir Guy Carleton landed his troops at Crown Point, and all eyes were turned to the lake shores as about to be the theatre of a decisive battle. Sir Guy approached Ticonderoga, as if designing to invest it, but "after reconnoitering the works, and observing the steady countenance of the garrison, he thought it too late to lay siege to the fortress. Re-embarking his army, he returned to Canada, where he placed it in winter quarters, making the Isle Aux Noix his most advanced post." Thus ended the Canadian invasion, and the operations on Lake Champlain were closed for the year 1776.

CHAPTER VIII.

Declaration of Independence by congress — Its effects — Anecdote of Colonel Skeen — Renewal of the difficulty with New York — Action of the New York convention — Counter-action in Vermont — Convention at Dorset — Resolutions to support the common cause — Preparations for a state government — Convention at Westminster — Vermont declaration of independence and memorial to Congress — Counter memorial from New York — Second New York memorial — Letter of Thomas Young to the inhabitants of Vermont — Third New York memorial — Rejection by congress of the petition of Vermont — Meeting in Vermont to adopt a constitution — Action upon the instrument reported — Abandonment of Ticonderoga by the American force and consequent alarm.

THE Declaration of Independence, by which the style of the confederacy was changed to the THIRTEEN UNITED STATES, did not come suddenly or unexpectedly upon the people. It had been debated and considered throughout the land, as the difficulties of maintaining the profession of allegiance while the colonies were in actual rebellion became more and more apparent, and the absurdity of such a position more evident. Great Britain exhibited no disposition to conciliate; the breach grew wider and wider; and although the timid feared, and some official steps had been taken in several of the state legislatures deprecating a "separation from our mother country," yet when the deed was formally done, men's minds were relieved. The questions which were presented became less complicated. All were narrowed down to the inquiry, how successful resistance of Great Britain could best be maintained.

But the New Hampshire grants, as Vermont was still called, were in a posture as difficult as ever. Colonel Skeen had obtained a commission from the British crown, and returned to endeavour to put it in force, though what extent of territory was proposed to annex to his government of Ticonderoga nobody knew. Probably, had he obtained this commission ten years before, he would have been discovered to be a man after the Green Mountain Boys' own heart. He was brave, bluff, facetious, and hard to intimidate. On his return from England, in 1775, he was taken into custody in Philadelphia, and retained for some time a prisoner, since he came with authority to raise a royal regiment. He was placed under guard at his lodgings, at the City Tavern; and Graydon, in his memoirs, relates the following amusing incident, of which he was an eye-witness. Skeen was to be removed from his lodgings, in Philadelphia, to a place of greater security, and the detailing of a guard for this purpose caused quite a crowd to assemble. The weather was warm, the windows were open, and Skeen, having finished his dinner, was discussing his wine and walnuts, while the guard politely waited his leisure. In compliment to his auditory, Skeen struck up "God save great George our king," in the voice of a stentor, and finished the song, highly to the amusement of the crowd, who thus got much more than they bargained for. Mr. Graydon, who afterward met him when their positions were changed, Graydon being a prisoner and Skeen among his friends, speaks in gratified terms of the staunch royalist's consideration and kindness. He seemed to be rather pleased than otherwise with the audacity of the rebels, having that sympathy with their courage which was natural to an old soldier who had seen service, and could appreciate daring. Such a man would have been a highly popular provincial governor for the Green Mountain Boys; and, as we shall presently see, he did not despair of that post.

New York, with wonderful tenacity, continued her claims upon the New Hampshire grants. After the formal severance of the colonies from Great Britain, the convention of the state of New York unanimously resolved "That all quit rents formerly due to the king of Great Britain, were now due and owing to this convention, or such future government as shall hereafter be established in this state." This was reviving the old colonial dispute in a most unbrotherly manner; for better things might have been expected of men engaged in the same heroic and perilous cause. The Green Mountain Boys were resolute in the determination not to submit to any such surrender of their rights, though to contend against New York would probably involve them in a contest with congress also. The course which had been taken upon their memorial to congress, showed them how little hope they had in that body against the influence which New York could bring; and yet to remain in their present condition seemed impossible.

While the great body of the people was resolute in maintaining a resistance to New York, there was a portion of the less daring who saw no other course but submission. Another party was in favour of joining New Hampshire, and claiming the protection of that state. But the leading minds, which always in times of danger influence the whole body, were clearly in favour of putting an end to the pretensions of New York by erecting the territory into an independent state. They saw no reason why the claims of Great Britain should fall to New York, by the severance of the colonies from the mother country, and reasoned that those claims or rights ceased, or became vested in the people of the grants. In order to produce concert, and to determine what was the view of the majority, a convention was called to meet at Dorset, July 24th, 1776. Thirty-five towns were represented in this convention, by fifty-one delegates. They agreed to support the Declaration of Independence, made by the Congress of the Thirteen United States, and to enter into an association among themselves for the defence of the country against Great Britain. But they firmly adhered to their former action against New York, and declared that any of the inhabitants of the New Hampshire grants, who should acknowledge the authority of New York, should be deemed enemies to the common cause. The convention proceeded carefully, and made their acts rather initiatory than final; being anxious to secure the cooperation of the whole people in a measure so important. The body adjourned to meet again in a month; and on the 25th of September, being again assembled, they resolved without any dissentient voice, "to take suitable measures, as soon as may be, to declare the New Hampshire grants a free and independent district." And the same body resolved that "no law or laws, direction or directions from the state of New York, should be accepted."

Having thus given the contemplated measure another degree of furtherance, the convention adjourned without day. The two meetings above referred to had been held at Dorset, on the west side of the mountains, where the people were most sensitive to the threatened aggressions of New York. The next convention was held at Westminster, on the east side of the Green Mountain range, celebrated for the collision with the sheriff and posse, mentioned in a preceding chapter. At this convention delegates were present from the towns in both sections of the territory. In the four months which had elapsed since the Dorset convention, the matter had been discussed and consulted upon in all its bearings, and the prevailing sentiment of the people was well understood. The proceedings of the convention were in unison with the popular voice. This body assembled on the 15th of January, 1777. Their proceedings look like foregone conclusions, for on the next day a declaration was unanimously adopted, which finally determined their attitude. The declaration was as follows:—

"This convention, whose members are duly chosen by the free voice of their constituents, in the several towns in the New Hampshire grants, in public meeting assembled, in our own names, and in behalf of our constituents, do hereby proclaim and publicly declare, that the district of territory comprehending, and usually known by the name of the New Hampshire grants, of right ought to be, and is hereby declared for ever hereafter to be considered as a free and independent jurisdiction or state; to be for ever hereafter called, known, and distinguished by the name of New Connecticut, *alias* Vermont. And that the inhabitants that at present, or that may hereafter become resident within said territory, shall be entitled to the same privileges, immunities, and enfranchisements which are, or that may at any time hereafter be allowed to the inhabitants of any of the free and independent states of America; and that such privileges and immunities shall be regulated in a Bill of Rights, and by a form of government to be established at the next session of the convention."

Having thus affirmed their independence, they drew up a memorial to congress. In this memorial they advised congress, as the representative of the United States, that they had taken their position as inhabitants of a free and independent state. They declared themselves capable of regulating their own internal police in all and every respect whatsoever; that they had the sole and exclusive right of governing themselves, in such manner and form as they themselves should choose, not repugnant to the resolves of Congress; and that they were at all times ready, in conjunction with their brethren in the United States, to contribute their full proportion toward the maintaining of the just war against the fleets and armies of Great Britain. And they prayed congress to recognise their state among the states in the Union, and to admit their delegates to a seat in congress. The petition was signed, and presented to congress, by four members of the convention, elected for that duty, Jonas Fay, Thomas Chittenden, Heman Allen, and Reuben Jones.

As might have been predicted, New York did not silently look on and suffer these proceedings to pass unopposed. The New England States were with Vermont in feeling, and whatever expression of opinion was heard in that quarter, was in favour of the Green Mountain Boys and their new government. But the New York convention lost no time in making an interest in congress adverse to the petition of Vermont. The president of that body, under date of January 20th, only four days from the date of the declaration of the Vermont convention, wrote thus to congress:

"I am directed by the committee of safety of New York, to inform congress that, by the acts and influence of certain designing men, a part of the state hath been prevailed on to revolt, and disown the authority of its legislature. The various evidences and informations we have received, would lead us to believe that persons of great influence in some of our sister states have fostered and fomented these divisions. But as these informations tend to accuse some members of your honourable body, of being concerned in this scheme, decency obliges us to suspend this belief. The committee are sorry to observe that by conferring a commission on Colonel Warner, with authority to name the officers of a regiment, to be raised independently of the legislature of this state, and within that part of it which hath lately declared an independence upon it, congress hath given but too much weight to the insinuations of those who pretend that your honourable body are determined to support those insurgents; especially as this Colonel Warner hath been constantly and invariably opposed to the legislature of this state, and hath been, on that very account, proclaimed an outlaw by the late government thereof. It is absolutely necessary to recall the commission given to Colonel Warner, and the officers under him, as nothing else will do justice to us, and convince those deluded people that congress has not been prevailed upon to aid in dismembering a state, which of all others has suffered the most in the common cause."

Again, on the 1st of March, the president of the New York convention addressed congress. In this memorial New York appealed to congress to adopt "every wise and salutary expedient to suppress the mischief which must ensue to that state, and the general confederacy, from the unjust and pernicious projects of such of the inhabitants of New York, as merely from selfish and interested motives have fomented the dangerous insurrection. That congress might be assured that the spirit of defection, notwithstanding all the arts and violence of the seducers, was by no means general, and that there was not the least probability that Colonel Warner could raise such a number of men as would be an object of public concern."

The affairs of the new state of Vermont had now arrested the attention of the whole country. We are not to suppose that the dispute between Vermont and New York was considered strictly upon its own merits; nor are we to think that the influence of New York was able to produce all the opposition, which took place in congress, to the reception of the new state. Other states as well as New York had their unsettled lands and backwoodsmen; and the danger which some politicians saw, was that new states would present themselves in other quarters, and the original bounds of the provinces be curtailed and their lands subdivided. It was a difficult matter to adjust, and every day seemed to add to the embarrassment. In April a paper appeared in Philadelphia, in the form of a letter, addressed to the inhabitants of Vermont. This pamphlet opened with a copy of the resolution passed by congress, in May, 1776, which recommended to the respective assemblies and conventions of the United Colonies, where no government suitable to the exigencies of their affairs had been established, to adopt such government as, in the opinion of the representatives of the people, should best conduce to the happiness and safety of their constituents.

The writer, Thomas Young, then went on to advise: "I have taken the minds of several leading members in the honourable the continental congress, and can assure you that you have nothing to do but to send attested copies of the recommendation to take up government to every township in your district, and to invite all your freeholders and inhabitants to meet in their respective townships, and choose members of a general convention, to meet on an early day, and choose delegates to the general congress; to appoint a committee of safety, and to form a constitution. Your friends here tell me that some are in doubt whether delegates from your district would be admitted into congress. I tell you to organize fairly and make the experiment, and I will insure your success, at the risk of my reputation as a man of honour or common sense. Indeed, they by no means refuse you; you have as good a right to choose how you will be governed, and by whom, as they had."

The committee of safety for the state of New York, now made a third appeal to congress. In this they stated that as a report prevailed, and daily gained credit, that the revolters against the jurisdiction of New York were privately countenanced in their designs by certain members of congress, the committee of safety felt it their duty to give such information on the subject, that congress might cease to be injured by imputations so disgraceful and dishonourable. "However unwilling," said the memorialists, "we may be to entertain suspicions so disrespectful to any member of congress, yet the truth is that no inconsiderable number of the people of this state do believe the report to be well founded."

Though exceedingly averse to meddle with a business so complicated, and conscious of its want of power to enforce any decision to which it might arrive, congress was compelled at last to take up the matter. One of the New York delegates laid before that body the printed letter of Thomas Young. Congress thus compelled to act, referred the several memorials and letters from New York and Vermont, and the printed paper signed Thomas Young, to the committee of the whole house, and on the 30th of June, a week after their reference, the committee reported, and congress passed, among others, a resolution that the petition of Vermont be *dismissed*.

The other resolutions defined the purpose of congress to be the defence of the colonies, now states, against Great Britain; and declared that as the members represented those states as their territories stood at the time of the first assembling of congress, that body would recommend or countenance nothing injurious to the rights of the communities it represented. They denied that the inhabitants of the New Hampshire grants could derive any countenance from the resolution quoted in Thomas Young's pamphlet; and they declared that the contents of the letter of Thomas Young were derogatory to the honour of congress, and a gross misrepresentation of the resolution of congress therein referred to, and that they tended to deceive the people to whom they were addressed. The commission of Colonel Warner was explained, but not recalled.

While these proceedings were taking place in congress, the inhabitants of Vermont were proceeding in the organization of the new state. The same convention which passed the declaration of the independence of Vermont, met by adjournment at Windsor, on the first Wednesday in June, and appointed a committee to draft a constitution for the state. They also adopted a resolution recommending the several towns to appoint delegates to meet in convention at Windsor, on the 2d of July, to act on the draft of the constitution which would be there submitted. Pursuant to this recommendation the convention assembled.

While the new constitution was under discussion, news arrived of the evacuation of Ticonderoga by the American troops, and of the consequent exposure of the whole western borders of Vermont to the enemy. Great alarm was felt at this intelligence, not only in Vermont, but in New York and Connecticut. The members of the convention partook of the feeling, and were for leaving Windsor, and repairing to the defence of their homes. Allen in his history of Vermont relates that the adjournment was postponed by a severe thunder storm. The members had time to reflect. Their attention was redirected to their work. The constitution was taken up and read the third time. Paragraph by paragraph was adopted. A committee of safety was appointed to act during the recess, and the convention adjourned in order. Quick upon the news of the loss of Ticonderoga, or simultaneously with it, came the intelligence of the dismissal of the petition by congress; but gallant little Vermont was neither driven from resistance to the foreign force or the domestic opponents.

CHAPTER IX.

Jealousies and disputes among the continental officers — Dislike of Schuyler by the New England troops — Schuyler tenders his resignation — Inquiry into his conduct — Honourable testimonial — Ordered to take command of the northern army — Carleton superseded by Burgoyne — Activity of Burgoyne — War feast with the Iroquois — Humane attempt of Burgoyne to restrain the barbarities of his Indian allies — Its futility — Manifesto to the Americans — Advance on Ticonderoga — Retreat of St. Clair — Death of Colonel Francis — Greenleaf's journal — Colonel Francis's watch restored to his mother — Concentration of American forces at Fort Edward — Burgoyne's halt at Skeensboro — Murder of Jane McCrea — The modern narrative — The popular version — Letter of Gates to Burgoyne — Reply of the latter.

NOT the least difficulty in the management of hostilities is found in the jealousies and disputes among the officers; the questions respecting precedence, and the sensitiveness of the military spirit to any thing like insult, oversight, or neglect. The safety of a country, or the efficiency of an army, cannot be sacrificed to the feelings of an officer, however meritorious. General Schuyler had the misfortune to be very unpopular with the New England troops; and reinforcements under him came forward with less spirit than the exigences of the service demanded. His demeanour to the officers of the New England regiments, whether retaliatory for their dislike to him, or the origin of that dislike, was a great disadvantage to the service. Probably prejudice against Schuyler as a New York officer had its effect. And the joint command of the operations of the war by Washington and the congress threw additional difficulties in the way. General Schuyler's head-quarters were, by a resolution of congress, March, 1776, fixed at Albany. This resolution, though he was nominally in command, precluded him from active service. As soon as the spring of 1777 opened, and the fear of an attack upon Ticonderoga, by a march over the ice, was removed, General Schuyler waited upon congress with the intention of offering his resignation. He demanded an inquiry into his conduct, which had been the subject of aspersion. A committee of one member from each state made the investigation, and the result was such as to show that the general's complaints of injustice had too much foundation. His services appeared of a character and importance which had never been duly appreciated; and as a measure of reparation the disagreeable resolution was rescinded, and General Schuyler was ordered to take command of the northern army. But the compliment to one was an insult to another—or was so regarded. General Gates withdrew in displeasure.

Meanwhile, there had also been a change in the British army. General Burgoyne, who had served under Sir Guy Carleton, had repaired to England with a report of the proceedings of the campaign in which the American forces were compelled to retreat. A plan for the invasion of the states, by way of the lakes, was arranged in London, and General Burgoyne, upon whose reports, and by whose counsel it was arranged, came back with orders superseding Sir Guy in the command. What that officer, who had so much distinguished himself in repelling invasion, would have accomplished in offensive operations, can only be subject of supposition; but the result of General Burgoyne's expedition proved most fortunate to the American cause. He had under his command a splendidly appointed army of not less than eight thousand men, exclusive of the Indians and Canadians, who were expected to join him, and for whom equipments were forwarded from England.

General Burgoyne entered upon his duty with a zeal and activity which indicated his confidence of success. On the 6th of May he landed at Quebec—on the 12th he proceeded to Montreal. On the 20th June he had already embarked a portion of his forces, and on the 21st landed on the New York side of Lake Champlain. His movements were made with such celerity as to make his presence so near the American posts almost a surprise. At this point he met the Indians of the Six Nations in a grand council, and gave them a war feast. The employment of such horrid allies is a disgrace to a Christian nation, and gives warfare, cruel enough at the best, additional features of atrocity. It is doubtless true that Burgoyne, while he urged the Indians to war, exhorted them to humanity; and while he put arms in their hands, endeavoured to teach them forbearance. But words weigh little against savage propensities. The savages followed their fiendish mode of warfare; and the exasperation which their conduct produced contributed no little to the zeal with which an enemy employing such aid was met. General Burgoyne indeed enjoined upon the

Indians that they were not to take scalps "from the wounded, or even from the dying," and professed to demand a strict account for those which were taken from the dead. But the weakness of making exceptions, while any scalps were suffered to be brought into his camp, is too apparent to need comment. Who was to answer the "strict inquiries," which General Burgoyne professed to make respecting these savage trophies of the Indians, which he admitted his inability to prevent them from taking!

After treating with his Indian allies, General Burgoyne commenced his operations with a manifesto, in which the pompous announcement of his titles was waggishly said, by contemporary American writers, to be more than a match for all the force of the United States. It was signed "By John Burgoyne, Esquire, Lieutenant-Governor of His Majesty's forces in America, Colonel of the Queen's Regiment of Light Dragoons, Governor of Fort William in North Britain, one of the Commons of Great Britain in Parliament, and Commanding an Army and Fleet employed on an Expedition from Canada." In this proclamation he enormously extolled the British might and his own, and did not forget the Indians. Of these men, whom, if we are to credit his assertions in a subsequent letter to General Gates "he had solemnly and peremptorily prohibited" from barbarity, he said, "I have but to give stretch to the Indian forces under my direction, and they amount to thousands, to overtake the hardened enemies of Great Britain and America. I consider them the same, wherever they may lurk." Unfortunately the Indians were not able or anxious always to distinguish "hardened enemies" from friends; and not a little damage was done to the royal cause from the insecurity of its provincial friends against Indian depredations.

Immediately upon the issue of his proclamation, General Burgoyne appeared before Ticonderoga. General Schuyler was absent from the fort, having repaired to Fort Edward, to hasten forward reinforcements and provisions. Every effort, consistent with the shortness of the time, had been made to strengthen the post, which was left in command of General St. Clair. On the 2d of July a skirmish took place with an American picket-guard, in which the British drove them in. The pursuers advanced within two hundred yards of the American batteries, of the precise location of which they seemed unaware. A random fire of artillery, without orders, killed only one man, and the smoke covered the retreat of the rest.

The fortress at Ticonderoga was deemed almost impregnable, and additional works had been thrown up on Mount Independence, a hill on the east side of Lake Champlain. But the works were nevertheless overlooked by a high hill, called Sugar Hill, or Mount Defiance. This eminence had not been fortified, for the double reason that it was considered impracticable, and that the Americans were not in force to man their present works properly. The garrison consisted of less than three thousand five hundred men. But to their surprise, on the 5th of July, they found the British erecting a battery on Sugar Hill, hoisting the cannon from tree to tree. This would command all the American works; and to escape complete investment, a retreat was resolved upon by the garrison, and effected on the night following. The invalids, and such baggage as could be removed, were embarked on board the batteaux for Skeensboro, now Whitehall. The main body proceeded by land, the rear-guard leaving Mount Independence at four o'clock, on the morning of the 6th of July.

The retreat would have been without disaster, but for a disobedience of orders. General St. Clair had required that nothing should be set on fire; but a French officer imprudently fired his house, and the flames illuminating the whole hill, showed the British the movements and designs of the Americans. General Burgoyne pursued the party by water, and Generals Frazer and Reidesel the main body by land. The American rear was commanded by Colonel Ebenezer Francis, of Beverly, Massachusetts, whose untimely death, in his thirty-fifth year, only prevented his winning a name as well known to the nation as it is dear to his descendants. We subjoin, from the "History of Beverly," by Mr. Stone, some particulars which will serve to show what material formed a portion of the Continental army, and also exhibit the circumstances of the retreat in graphic language.

Colonel Francis marched at the head of his regiment from Massachusetts to Ticonderoga, in January, 1777. With that regard for religion which was the characteristic of his life, he assembled the regiment for religious services, in his own parish church, previous to his march. His pastor, who conducted the services, which were of a most solemn and impressive character, accompanied the regiment as chaplain. Captain Greenleaf, whose private journal is preserved in the library of the Massachusetts Historical Society, thus records the circumstances of the retreat: —

63

"14th June, heard enemy's morning gun—Indians and others near—skirmishes. 2d July, enemy advances with two frigates of twenty-eight guns, and fifty gun-boats—land troops about two miles from us. Saturday, July 5th, at twelve o'clock, spied British troops on the mountain overlooking Ticonderoga—at nine received the disagreeable news of leaving the ground. At two next morning left Ticonderoga—at four, Mount Independence; after a most fatiguing march, arrived same day at Hubbardton, near Whitehall, twenty-two miles from Mount Independence. Supped with Col. Francis—encamped in the woods, the main body going on about four miles. Monday, 7th July, breakfasted with Col. F. At seven, he came to me and desired me to parade the regiment, which I did. At a quarter past seven he came in haste to me, told me an express had arrived from General St. Clair, informing that we must march with the greatest expedition, or the enemy would be upon us, also that they had taken Skeensboro, with all our baggage—ordered me to march the regiment—immediately marched a part of it. At twenty minutes past seven, the enemy appeared in gunshot of us; we faced to the right and the firing began, which lasted till a quarter to nine without cessation. Numbers fell on both sides; among ours the brave and ever to be lamented Col. Francis, who fought bravely to the last. He first received a ball through his right arm, but still continued at the head of our troops, till he received a fatal wound through his body, entering his right breast; he dropped on his face. Our people being overpowered by numbers, were obliged to retreat over the mountains, enduring in their march great privations and sufferings."

Thus died Colonel Francis, of whom a British officer who was in the engagement thus speaks: "At the commencement of the action the enemy were everywhere thrown into the greatest confusion; but being rallied by that brave officer, Colonel Francis, whose death, though an enemy, will ever be regretted by those who can feel for the loss of a gallant and brave man, the fight was renewed with the greatest degree of fierceness and obstinacy."

It is a curious fact that the officer who thus records the death of Colonel Francis, afterward met his mother, and was witness to a most affecting interview. He was a prisoner with General Burgoyne, near Boston, on parole, and while walking with other British officers in the like case, stopped with them at a farm-house. An elderly woman who was sitting in the house, recognised them as British officers. "Just as we were quitting the house," says the narrator, "she got up, and bursting into tears, said, 'Gentlemen, will you let a poor distracted woman speak a word to you before you go?' We, as you must all naturally imagine, were all astonished; and upon our inquiring what she wanted, with the most poignant grief, and sobbing as if her heart was breaking, she asked if any of us knew her son, a Colonel Francis, who was killed at the battle of Hubbardton. Several of us informed her that we had seen him after he was dead. She then inquired about his pocket-book, and if any of his papers were safe, as some related to his estates, and if any of the soldiers had got his watch; if she could but obtain that in remembrance of her dear, dear son, she should be happy. Captain Ferguson, of our regiment, who was of the party, told her, as to the colonel's papers and pocket-book, he was fearful they were either lost or destroyed; but pulling a watch from his fob, he said, 'There, good woman, if that can make you happy, take it, and God bless you!' We were all much surprised, as unacquainted he had made a purchase of it from a drum boy. On seeing it, it is impossible to describe the joy and grief that were depicted in her countenance. I never in all my life beheld such a strength of passion; she kissed it, looked unutterable gratitude at Captain Ferguson, then kissed it again; her feelings were unexpressible; she knew not how to express or to show them; she would repay his kindness by kindness, but could only sob her thanks. Our feelings were lifted up to an unexpressible height. We promised to search after the papers, and I believe at that moment could have hazarded life to procure them."

Such strange incidents does war, that anomaly amid civilization, furnish!

Colonel Warner, with his Green Mountain regiment, was with Colonel Francis. We need hardly say that this regiment stood their ground manfully. After the fall of Francis, Warner charged with such impetuosity that for a moment the British troops were thrown into confusion. But a reinforcement arriving, the Americans were completely overpowered. Two or three regiments, which should have been in the engagement, consulted their own safety by a retreat; and the rout of the rest was complete. The loss of the Americans was very severe, amounting to between three and four hundred men, killed, wounded, and prisoners.

The retreating army collected at Fort Edward, having lost all their baggage and stores. General Burgoyne destroyed in a few hours the water defences at Ticonderoga, and pushed on to Skeensboro, where the garrison attempted no stand, but setting fire to the mills and bateaux, retreated. They were pursued, but defended themselves with so much spirit that the pursuit was given over, and General Burgoyne halted a few days at Skeensboro, to refresh his men.

It was during the subsequent advance upon Fort Edward that the murder of Miss Jane McCrea roused the resentment of the Americans to the highest degree; and, in the excitement of the times, covered General Burgoyne with unmerited obloquy. This tragical story belongs to the romance of the Revolutionary war; and, while the people were filled with horror and indignation, that narrative which reflected the greatest dishonour upon the British commander and his savage allies was accepted as most likely to be the true one. Now, however, when party feeling has subsided, a calmer investigation of the circumstances connected with that hapless affair has led to the belief that the popular version is incorrect in many important particulars.

Jane McCrea was the affianced bride of a Mr. Jones, a young American, of loyalist principles, who had joined Burgoyne, and accepted a commission in the British army. Little doubt was entertained, at that period, of the eventual success of the royal cause. The progress of the invading force under Burgoyne had hitherto been a most triumphant one. When the British approached Fort Edward, Miss McCrea was the guest of Mrs. McNeil, whose house was at the foot of a hill, distant about eighty rods northward from the fort. "The hill-side was covered with bushes, while a quarter of a mile above, near the crest of the hill, a large pine tree shadowed a clear spring."

The brother with whom Jenny had previously lived, being a staunch Whig, was preparing to abandon his house, five miles below the fort, and retire to Albany. Apprehensive of danger to his sister, he several times desired her to join him without delay. The hope of meeting her lover causing her still to linger, her brother became alarmed, and despatched so peremptory a message that she promised to return to his house the following day.

The next morning, the negro boy belonging to Mrs. McNeil hurriedly informed the family of the approach of a small party of Indian warriors, and then fled across the plain to the fort for protection. Acting on the impulse of the moment, the whole family hastily sought refuge in the cellar of a kitchen detached from the house. While crouching here in the darkness, the colour of the servant woman shielded her from discovery, but Mrs. McNeil and Jenny were seized, and hurried off by different routes to Burgoyne's camp. In the mean time, a detachment had been sent out from Fort Edward to attempt a rescue; and when the party who were bearing off Jenny approached the pine tree and the spring near the summit of the hill, they were suddenly fired upon by the American pursuers. During the brief skirmish that followed, Jenny was accidentally struck by a bullet, and fell from her horse mortally wounded. Her Indian captors, conscious that by her death they had lost the reward usually paid for prisoners, could not forego the barbarous temptation of bearing off her scalp as a trophy. It was taken, and carried by them openly displayed into camp, where the long glossy hair of Jenny was speedily recognised by Mrs. McNeil, who boldly taxed the Indians with the murder of her guest. They promptly denied it, and asserted that she came by her death in the manner already described.

Information subsequently obtained tended to confirm the truth of this statement, notwithstanding a different version of the tragical story has usually prevailed. The latter narrative charges Lieutenant Jones with having bribed the Indians with a promise of rum to conduct his betrothed into the British lines; that as they returned with their fair captive, a quarrel arose respecting the division of the liquor, and, to end the dispute, one of the Indians despatched Jenny by shooting her through the breast. But Lieutenant Jones strenuously denied having engaged the services of the Indians at all; nor is it probable he would do so, inasmuch as the British army was then advancing upon Fort Edward, with the certainty of its capture. The young officer could, therefore, have no desire for the presence of Miss McCrea in camp, especially as, in a day or two, the possession of Fort Edward would have enabled him to visit her with greater comfort and security at the house of their mutual friend, Mrs. McNeil.

Overcome with horror at her terrible fate, Jones tendered immediately a resignation of his commission. Burgoyne refusing to accept it, he deserted. Retiring to Canada, bearing with him the blood-stained tresses of his affianced bride, he lived there for many years. He never married, shunned all allusion to the War of Independence, kept rigidly the anniversary of Miss McCrea's death; and became, from the period of his bereavement, a sad, thoughtful, and secluded man.

The popular version of this melancholy event, at the time of its occurrence, we may presume to have been something like the following, which we extract from a letter written to General Burgoyne by General Gates, in answer to one in which General Burgoyne complained of certain alleged harsh treatment of prisoners. "Miss McCrea, a young lady lovely to the sight, of virtuous character and amiable disposition, engaged to an officer of your army, was, with other women and children, taken out of a house near Fort Edward, carried into the woods, and there scalped and mangled in the most shocking manner. Two parents with their six children were all treated with the same inhumanity, while quietly resting in their once peaceful and happy dwelling. The miserable fate of Miss McCrea was particularly aggravated by being dressed to receive her promised husband, but met her murderer appointed by you. Upward of one hundred men, women, and children have perished by the hands of the ruffians to whom, it is asserted, you have paid the price of blood."

General Burgoyne, in his reply, inveighs against "the rhapsodies of fiction and calumny" which it had been, he alleged, the invariable policy of the Americans to propagate. But with all the elements of a fearfully tragic and romantic story, which the death of Miss McCrea furnished, Americans must have been different from all other people, if the narrative did not grow with the repetition. They must have been insensible to murder and cruelty, could they have weighed all the rumours and dispassionately sifted out truth from error. The disgrace which the British allies entailed upon their employers was a part of the price of their service—nowhere better understood than by indignant statesmen at home, as the remonstrances of the opposition in Parliament testify.

CHAPTER X.

Action of Vermont and New Hampshire upon the fall of Ticonderoga — Orders of General Stark — Resolves in Congress — Schuyler's judicious measures — General Burgoyne's second proclamation — Vain appeal of Major Skeene — General Stark's insubordination — Resolution of censure in Congress — British attempt to secure the stores at Bennington — Battle of Bennington — Attack on Colonel Baum's entrenchments — Complete success of General Stark — Renewal of the engagement by Colonels Warner and Breyman — Defeat of the latter — Important effects upon the American cause — Extract from Burgoyne's instructions to Colonel Baum — General Burgoyne's opinion of the people of the New Hampshire grants — Appointment of Gates to supersede Schuyler — General Gates arrives at Stillwater — Battle of Stillwater or Behmus Heights — Victory claimed by both parties, but the real advantage with the Americans — Battle of the 7th October — General Burgoyne retreats to Saratoga — Capitulation of Burgoyne.

WHEN the disastrous intelligence of the fall of Ticonderoga reached the Vermont council of safety, they despatched pressing letters to New Hampshire and Massachusetts, setting forth their exposed condition, and urging those states for assistance. The New Hampshire council immediately convened the legislature, and that body placing a large force under command of General Stark, directed him to repair to Charleston, on the Connecticut River, and there consult with the Vermont council as to the forwarding of supplies, and the conduct of future operations. He was instructed to act in conjunction with the troops of Vermont, or any other state, or of the United States, in such manner as, in his opinion, would most effectually stop the operations of the enemy. This very broad exercise of discretion was given him in consequence of his independent position; for disgusted with the neglect with which he conceived himself treated, in not being made a brigadier-general in the Continental army, Stark had just resigned his commission as colonel, and conceiving himself not amenable to command in the regular army, he had stipulated for this independent command. This was another of the many difficulties which Congress had with its officers; but in the result it proved a fortunate circumstance.

The news of the Ticonderoga disaster caused amazement every where, and no little indignation. In Congress the retreat was made the subject of warm animadversion; and the recall of all the officers was ordered, and only suspended on the earnest expostulation of General Washington against leaving the northern army without officers. Subsequent inquiry, and a revelation of the comparative weakness of the garrison and the strength of the besiegers, caused the officers to be exonerated from all blame.

General Schuyler, who, as previously stated, was absent forwarding supplies when Ticonderoga was taken, was on his return when he heard of the fall of that important post, and of the loss of Skeensboro. He set about immediately staying the mischief with a fortitude and industry most commendable, and employed the forced respite which Burgoyne gave him, in destroying bridges, breaking up roads, sinking obstructions in the navigable creeks, and felling trees across the road. So effectually was this work done, that when the British army moved forward from Skeensboro, they were often occupied twenty-four hours in advancing one mile. The horses and draught cattle were driven off, and the passage of the British from Skeensboro to Fort Edward on the Hudson, delayed them until the 29th of July. General Schuyler had meanwhile crossed the river and retreated first to Saratoga, and then to Stillwater, where he encamped on a rising ground called Behmus Heights.

General Burgoyne now issued a second proclamation. As the petition of Vermont for admission into the Union had been so cavalierly treated, the British general counted the juncture a good one to establish Skeene's new province, and summoned delegates to meet at Castleton, to confer with the gallant major on that subject. But Governor Skeene's title never was acknowledged in any instrument except his commission and Burgoyne's proclamation. Unkindly as the Green Mountain Boys conceived themselves to have been treated, they were not yet ready for the royal protection; and the only effect which Burgoyne's proclamation produced, was to call out a counter-manifesto from General Schuyler.

The disasters which had so dispirited the American army now began to change to the British. The Americans were reinforced, and their spirits were raised by the defeat of an attempt of the British and Indians to seize Fort

Schuyler, at the western boundary of the New York settlements. The Indian allies deserted the British, and after one or two brilliant skirmishes the siege was raised.

General Stark had now at Manchester a force of 1400 men, 600 of whom were Green Mountain Boys, under Colonel Warner. Schuyler wrote to him repeatedly to join the main army; but Stark, in pursuance of the discretion allowed to him by his New Hampshire commission, chose to remain where he was. Schuyler represented this insubordination to Congress; and on the 19th of August that body passed a resolution censuring the course pursued by New Hampshire, in giving General Stark a separate command, and requesting that he should be instructed to conform himself to the same rules to which other general officers of the militia were subject.

General Stark, whose patriotism outweighed his resentment, while he moved toward the post indicated by General Schuyler, still moved at his leisure. He was with his regiment at Bennington, longing for an opportunity to do something upon his own account, when an occasion presented itself. Burgoyne had found his position attended with great difficulties. His supplies from Canada were irregular, and not one-third of the horses on which he had counted had arrived. The judicious measures of General Schuyler had so consumed the time of the British army, that their stores were nearly expended; and, as he was compelled to keep the road open behind him to forward provisions, the detachments necessary for this purpose weakened his army for active operations. In this difficulty a supply must be had from some source. A depot of provisions and other stores was established at Bennington for the American army, and with this Burgoyne proposed to replenish his magazines. It was reported to be guarded only by militia, and the sentiments of a majority of the residents were furthermore stated to be hostile to the American cause. We are not in possession of absolute facts for the opinion, but it seems exceedingly probable that the irritation of the Green Mountain Boys at their treatment by Congress may have given rise to expressions which induced Burgoyne to doubt their attachment to the United States.

Colonel Baum, with five hundred European troops, some American loyalists and Indian auxiliaries, was detached on this service. Another detachment under Colonel Breyman was advanced as a reserve. General Stark, at Bennington, heard of the approach of a body of Indians, and despatched a detachment under Colonel Greg, to arrest their proceedings. It was soon discovered that these savages were the advance party of Colonel Baum's command. General Stark instantly sent an express to Colonel Warner, to hasten to his aid, and also called upon the militia of the vicinity to join him with all possible despatch.

On the morning of the 14th of August, General Stark, with the force at his command, advanced to meet Colonel Baum, and on the way met Colonel Greg in retreat before the enemy. Stark immediately formed in order of battle, and Colonel Baum perceiving that the Americans were in too great strength to be attacked by his present force, halted, and despatched an express to Colonel Breyman for assistance. General Stark finding his position unfavourable for an engagement, chose a better position, about a mile in the rear. Here it was resolved in a council of war attack to Baum at once, before he could receive reinforcements, and the next day was appointed for the engagement. That day, however, proved rainy; and beyond frequent skirmishes of small parties, in which the spirits of the Americans were much raised by success, nothing was done. Baum, meanwhile, improved the delay to intrench himself in his camp, and fortify his position. The rain and the state of the roads delayed Breyman's march.

On the morning of the 16th, General Stark, having been joined by some Massachusetts militia, determined on an attack, although Colonel Warner had not yet arrived. Drawing out his forces, he made the very brief speech to them which is familiar to all readers of American history: "Boys, there they are! We beat to-day, or Sally Stark's a widow!" The attack on the entrenchments was made in four points at once. It is stated by some authorities, that so confident were the Tory provincials under Baum's command, of the attachment of the country to the royal cause, that while Stark was making dispositions for an attack, they supposed his men to be armed loyalists, coming to join them.

This error was soon discovered. The four divisions, numbering in all about eight hundred men, made their attack almost simultaneously. The Indian allies of the British, with their characteristic poltroonery, where hard fighting and no plunder was the prospect, fled at the commencement of the attack. The German troops fought like lions, and when their ammunition was expended, rushed to the charge, led by their gallant leader, Colonel Baum. After two hours of close and severe contest the victory was complete, and the whole British detachment, except the Indians and the loyalists, who took to the woods, were either killed or taken prisoners.

Just as Stark's men had fallen into the confusion of victory, which is scarcely less than that of defeat, the alarm was given that Colonel Breyman was rapidly approaching. Fortunately, at this precise juncture, Colonel Warner also arrived; and the two bodies of reserve, not reaching in season to join the first encounter, renewed the battle. General Stark collected his men, and hastened to the assistance of Warner. The battle was continued till sunset, when the British force gave way, abandoning their baggage and artillery. The Americans pursued them until dark, and thus closed the famous battle of Bennington—a victory most opportune, and the prelude of more successes.

The American loss was only fourteen killed, and forty-two wounded. The British loss was about two hundred killed, and over six hundred prisoners, a thousand stand of arms, four pieces of artillery, and a thousand dragoon swords. But the moral effect of such success was a great deal the most important. The prestige of invincibility with which the timid had begun to invest the British army was taken from it; and the trained soldiers of Europe were taught how raw troops could fight for their altars and firesides. The patriotism of Vermont was vindicated, and the hope of the enemy in the defection of the settlers was dissipated. How sanguine this expectation was on the part of Burgoyne, may be judged from Colonel Baum's instructions, a copy of which fell into the hands of General Stark. These instructions directed Colonel Baum to "proceed through the New Hampshire grants, cross the mountains with Peter's corps, (levies,) and the Indians, from Rockingham to Otter Creek; to get horses, carriages, and cattle, and mount Reidesel's dragoons; to go down Connecticut River as far as Brattleboro, and return by the great road to Albany, there to meet General Burgoyne; to endeavour to make the country believe it was the advance body of the general's army, who was to cross Connecticut River and proceed to Boston; and that at Springfield they were to be joined by the troops from Rhode Island. All officers, civil and military, acting under Congress, to be made prisoners. To tax the towns where they halted for such articles as they wanted, and to take hostages for the performance. To bring all horses fit to mount the dragoons, or to serve as battalion horses for the troops, with as many saddles and bridles as can be found. The number of horses requisite, besides those for the dragoons, ought to be thirteen hundred; if you can bring more, so much the better. The horses must be tied in strings of ten each, so that one man may lead ten horses," &c. &c.

We question whether instructions ever fell farther short of fulfilment than did those of the unfortunate Colonel Baum. We have quoted them to show what an egregiously false estimate General Burgoyne had formed of the character of the inhabitants and of the resources of the country. The news of the failure of the attack upon Fort Schuyler close following upon the Bennington defeat, very much depressed the spirits of the royal army. In a private letter of Burgoyne's, dated August 20th, he says: "The New Hampshire grants in particular, a country unpeopled and almost unknown in the last war, now abound in the most active and most rebellious race on the continent, who hang like a gathering storm upon my left." As the confidence of the British decreased, that of the Americans was restored, and recruits now came into the American camp in large numbers.

At the time of the passage of the resolution in Congress recalling the general officers in the northern army, General Washington was requested to name a successor to General Schuyler. The commander-in-chief declined to make the nomination, and Congress appointed General Gates. General Schuyler very keenly felt this mortification, but with a magnanimity which does him high honour he continued his exertions in forwarding the operations of the campaign. His services in retrieving or arresting the disasters which followed the loss of Ticonderoga, though necessarily of a nature to give him no public eclat, were of vast advantage to his country; and although his personal unpopularity with the New England men made his removal from the command a matter of expedience, if not of necessity, his services are not now overlooked by his countrymen.

General Gates arrived at Stillwater, and assumed the command on the 19th of August, just at the time when the turning tide made every thing propitious for the American cause. He instantly availed himself of his advantages, and being seconded by large bodies of volunteers, eager for service, soon reduced the condition of Burgoyne to the defensive. The New England militia, under the command of General Lincoln, surprised all the outposts of the enemy on Lake George, except Ticonderoga, taking nearly three hundred prisoners, liberating a hundred Americans, and destroying what munitions, boats, and stores they could not carry away. Their loss in these affairs was only three killed and five wounded. As Burgoyne moved, detachments of the Americans, principally militia and volunteers, were constantly cutting off his supplies, and breaking up his lines of communication. On the 13th and 14th of September he crossed the Hudson, and advanced toward the American army. To prevent being cut off in detail, it had become necessary that he should decide the fate of the campaign in a general engagement.

The Americans as they retreated had blocked roads and destroyed bridges, and the advance of General Burgoyne was necessarily slow, the strength and patience of his soldiers being sorely tried by these delays and difficulties. Desertions now became frequent, from the refugee or provincial regiments, who began to discover the mistake into which they had fallen.

On the 19th of September occurred the memorable battle of Stillwater. Burgoyne had advanced and encamped within four miles of the American lines. There appears to have been a well-weighed hesitancy on both sides, as to hazarding a battle. The Americans respected the discipline and courage of the foreign troops; and the British commander felt like a man at bay, confident of his desperate courage, but fearful that it would avail him little. On the 18th, the show of challenge was made by the Americans. On the 19th, the same course was taken by Burgoyne. The accidental meeting of two scouting parties brought on the general engagement which the respective commanders had desired, and yet hesitated to provoke. General Burgoyne at the head of the right wing of the British army, advanced toward the left of the Americans, while another detachment menaced their right. An accidental encounter precipitated the meeting of the two armies.

No sooner was the firing of the scouts heard, than the advanced parties of each army pressed forward. The events of the day are thus graphically summed by Thompson, in his History of Vermont: "Reinforcements were continually sent on upon both sides, and the engagement became obstinate and general. The first attempt of the Americans was to turn the right wing of the British army, and flank their line. Failing in this, they moved in regular order to the left, and there made a furious assault. Both armies were determined to conquer, and the battle raged without intermission for three hours. Any advantage upon one side was soon counterbalanced by an equal advantage on the other. Cannon, and favourable positions were taken, lost, and retaken in quick succession; and the two armies might be compared to the two scales of a mighty balance, trembling with equal burdens in doubtful oscillation, and, had not night put an end to the contest, it is doubtful which would have preponderated." It appears from collating the accounts of the battle, that each army succeeded best in repelling attacks. Assailing parties were vigorously resisted, but when pursued to the lines, the pursuers in turn were driven back. Both parties claimed the victory, and each believed itself to have been engaged with only a part of its own force with nearly the whole of the enemy. The loss of the Americans was sixty-four killed, and two hundred and sixty wounded and missing. The loss of the British has been estimated at rather more than five hundred men, killed, wounded, and prisoners. The Americans returned to their camp; the British slept upon the ground.

The victory was claimed by the British since they had retained possession of the field, but the Americans asserted the same claim. Whatever may be the technical answer to the problem, the solid advantage was with the Americans. To the British general any thing less than a decisive victory was a defeat. To the Americans, the check to the advancing army which they had effected, was a victory. But of far greater consequence was the impression which the heroic conduct of the Americans made upon the British forces. The impromptu soldiers, whom they despised as "forever unworthy of their steel," had astonished them by their fierce bravery and resolute conduct. The desertion of provincials, Canadians, and Indians from Burgoyne now increased, and he was driven to the conclusion that his European soldiers were the only men upon whom he could place any reliance.

On the next day after the battle, General Burgoyne changed his position to one almost within cannon-shot of the American camp, and fortified himself there, keeping his communication with the river open. Thus the two armies remained from the 20th of September, until the 7th of October; the American army constantly receiving accessions, and the British continually diminishing. The force now at Gates's command enabled him to post detachments in all the avenues of escape or retreat, and General Burgoyne's position became most critical. He still hoped for aid from Sir Henry Clinton, who was forcing his way up the Hudson; but having only a few days' provision in camp, he was compelled again to try his strength with the Americans. He put himself at the head of fifteen hundred regulars, to cover the operations of a foraging party.

General Gates immediately made his dispositions for an attack, and assailed General Burgoyne at three points at once, and almost succeeded in cutting off his return to his camp. Overpowered by numbers, and with the loss of his field-pieces, and a great part of his artillery corps, Burgoyne with difficulty retreated to his entrenchments. Two hundred prisoners, and nine pieces of cannon were taken by the Americans. A part of the British works was also carried, and when night put an end to the battle, the Americans remained in possession. The whole loss of the British was four hundred men, in killed, wounded, and prisoners, and among the dead and wounded were several officers of note. Arnold, who was conspicuous in the American line, though without a command, was badly wounded in leading an assault within the entrenchments.

No more military operations of consequence occurred. General Burgoyne, in the night after the battle, withdrew from the works, which were partly in the possession of the Americans, and drew up his army in the order of battle on some high grounds in the rear. From this position he was compelled to retreat to avoid being surrounded, and accordingly on the night of the 8th of October he removed again, and on the evening of the next day reached Saratoga. The project of abandoning the baggage, and with arms in hand forcing a retreat to Canada, was discussed, but upon examination found impracticable. Hemmed in on all hands, Burgoyne had no choice but surrender, which he did on the 16th of October. He was allowed to march out of camp with the honours of war. General Gates, being advised of the progress of the relief designed for Burgoyne, pressed the capitulation, without making difficulty about terms; and the victors treated the vanquished with the most considerate kindness. The prisoners were five thousand, six hundred and forty-two. The previous losses of the British had been nearly four thousand; and thus was this fine army, which entered the country with such an imposing front, completely disposed of.

The British garrison at Ticonderoga retreated at once to Canada. The expedition to relieve Burgoyne, which had advanced up the river within fifty miles of Albany, fell back to New York, upon hearing of Burgoyne's capitulation. General Gates was ordered to other points with the regular army, the volunteers returned to their homes, and the country in Vermont and vicinity was no more the scene of any important operations during the War of the Revolution. While having less to attach themselves to the cause than any other part of the country, and contending with single states and with the United States for their very existence, the inhabitants of Vermont showed a constancy in their patriotism which entitled them to the highest honour. We have already quoted the testimony of General Burgoyne to their character. In the capture of the British army, they performed an important part, as they had previously done in the invasion of Canada by the American forces.

CHAPTER XI.

Delay in the organization of the Vermont state government — Reassembling of the convention — Recognition by New Hampshire — First election of assemblymen — Continued opposition of New York — Proclamation of Governor Clinton — Steady course of Vermont — Answer of Ethan Allen to Governor Clinton — Constitution of Vermont — Its original features — Modifications — Simple forms of legislation — Governor Chittenden — Anecdote of the Landlord Governor — Biographical notice — Summary of his character — First meeting of the Vermont legislature — Embarrassing proposals from sixteen towns in New Hampshire — Adjournment of the legislators to consult their constituents — The sixteen towns received into union — Remonstrance of New Hampshire — Appeals to Congress — Colonel Ethan Allen visits Philadelphia to consult with the members — New York difficulty — Vermont hesitates to perfect the union — Secession of a portion of her legislators — They convene to form a new state — Vermont cuts off the sixteen towns — New Hampshire and New York each claim the whole of her territory — Interference of Massachusetts.

PREVIOUS to its adjournment, the convention which met at Windsor in July, 1777, appointed a day in December following, for the election of representatives, to meet at Windsor in January. But the invasion of Burgoyne so much occupied people's thoughts and attention that the constitution was not printed in season for the people to understand and hold their first meeting under it. Many of the frontier settlements of Vermont were broken up after the retreat of the Americans from Canada, in 1776, and during the confusion of the following year. It is remarkable that the new state kept up even the form of organization at such a crisis, and amid such confusion. It was only done by perfect confidence in the leaders, and by their worthiness of the trust reposed in them. The council of safety, finding that the election could not take place at the time appointed, called together again the convention which had framed the constitution. That body assembled, revised the instrument which they had passed at the former meeting, and directed the first election under it to take place in March following, and the first meeting of the legislature in the same month. The election and the legislative session took place accordingly, the constitution going into effect without the form of ratification by the people. New Hampshire recognised the new order of things, almost before the people of Vermont. Upon the alarm occasioned by the fall of Ticonderoga, which occurred while the convention which framed the constitution was still in session, when an appeal was made to New Hampshire for aid, the executive of that state, in a letter addressed to Vermont as a free, sovereign, but new state, recognised the new commonwealth.

New York was not, however, disposed to relinquish jurisdiction so readily. The vexed question of land titles, and the pledged protection of the state to certain holders under her grants were in the way, as also, no doubt, some pride. In February, 1778, while the election of the Vermont legislature was pending, the governor of New York issued a proclamation, affirming certain land titles, and adopting a more conciliatory tone than had been the custom under the royal regime; but still declaring, in reference to the resistants, that New York would "vigorously maintain its rightful supremacy over the persons and property of those disaffected subjects." Little Vermont, however, unawed by threats, was equally invulnerable to mingled threats and cajolery; and having taken her stand, was resolved to maintain it. In the spring of this year (1778) Ethan Allen returned from his forced foreign travels, and his detention as prisoner in his own country; and he made early use of his pen by publishing an answer to the New York proclamation, in which he declared that its overtures were "all romantic, designed only to deceive backwoods people."

The original constitution of Vermont had many peculiarities which have been since abandoned. It was thoroughly democratic, extending suffrage in a far more liberal spirit than any other of the states. Every man twenty-one years of age, who had resided a year in the state previous to the election, was entitled to vote. The executive power was originally vested in a governor, lieutenant-governor, and a council of twelve, elected at the time when the representatives were chosen. The legislature consisted of one body only, called the assembly, the members of which were required to make a subscription to a belief in God, and the inspiration of the Scriptures, and to make a profession of the Protestant faith. Each town had one representative, and no more. The council could suggest amendments in the acts passed, but had no legislative power, and no absolute veto. Every law was at first required to lie over one session, except in urgent cases, and be printed for the information of the people. Schools in every town were required by the constitution. No person, born in this country or brought from over sea, could be held in servitude or apprenticeship, except for crime or debt, unless by their own consent after reaching majority. A council of thirteen censors was chosen every thirteen years to inquire into violations of the constitution, and recommend amendments if necessary; but their office would seem to have been nearly a sinecure, so far as amendments were concerned.

In 1785 a revision took place, in which the requirement that laws should lay over a year was abandoned, except in cases where the governor and council objected to any portion. At the same revisal, the requirement of a Protestant faith in the representatives was stricken out; and at another revision, in 1793, all religious subscription was abolished. For nearly fifty years the constitution remained unaltered, except in the introduction of an article providing for the naturalization of foreigners; but in 1836 Vermont accommodated her mode of legislation to that of the other states, and abolishing the council of twelve, adopted a senate of thirty members in its stead. Pennsylvania had tried, and early abandoned the plan of a one-house legislature; and it is remarkable that Franklin was an earnest advocate for a system which experience has proved inconvenient, if not impracticable. The other important provisions of the constitution remain as in the beginning. The judiciary is elected by the legislature. The expenses of the government of Vermont are upon the most frugal scale possible; and her laws are fewer in number, and less in bulk, than those of any other state in the Union.

Thomas Chittenden, chosen governor of Vermont at the first election in 1778, held that office by annual re-election for eighteen years; and during the whole term of his gubernatorial service continued his occupation of farmer and innkeeper. It is related that a stranger from another state, having business with the governor, overtook a farmer driving a load of hay, and inquired of him the way to the residence of that official. The farmer answered that it was a short distance, and he was going directly there; and the stranger walked his horse behind the wagon, until it stopped at an inn. The farmer inquired if the horse of the traveller was to be fed, and receiving a reply in the affirmative, attended to the animal. He next directed his boys to take charge of the hay. Then, taking off his farmer's frock, and washing his hands and head, he turned to the waiting stranger: "Now then, what is it you want of the governor?" Such practical republicanism could not fail to be popular, since it was natural, simple, and unaffected.

Governor Chittenden was a native of Guilford, in Connecticut, and having early filled many posts of trust in his native state, he removed to the New Hampshire grants in 1774. He had followed the custom always prevalent in unartificial communities, and early taken to himself a wife. With her and his infant children he established himself on the borders, in the township of Williston, and was in the successful pursuit of his peaceful occupations when the difficulties with Great Britain commenced. He was appointed one of a committee sent to Philadelphia, in 1775, to procure intelligence of the measures which Congress intended to pursue, and to take advice as to the course which should be adopted by the people of the New Hampshire grants.

Upon the retreat of the American army from Canada, in 1776, Mr. Chittenden, with others in the border towns, was compelled to withdraw to escape the ravages of war and Indian treachery. He took up his temporary abode in Arlington, and became at once one of the most prominent men in the affairs of the state. He was president of the council of safety, and his practical knowledge was very useful to his compatriots in the management of their complicated business. Mr. Chittenden was one of the earliest advocates for a separate state government, as the best mode of determining the complicated questions of jurisdiction, raised by New York and New Hampshire. This purpose he steadily pursued until he saw Vermont acknowledged by the neighbouring states, and admitted as a member of the Federal Union. He was a member of the convention which framed the state government, and indeed was identified with all the measures of importance undertaken by the people of Vermont while he lived, which was to the appointed limit—"three score years and ten." As governor he kept down party spirit by his moderation and calmness; and the want of a liberal education, which must in some situations operate as a great disadvantage, in the case of Governor Chittenden was perhaps a decided benefit to the interests of the state. In his day no gubernatorial speech or message opened the sessions of the assembly, but the legislators proceeded directly to the business, which their modest pay—six shillings currency per day—did not tempt them to prolong, or needlessly to make intricate. The governor's salary was on the same modest scale, being originally fixed at £150 per annum; and the whole proceedings of this truly republican body were marked by the utmost simplicity and plainness.

The narrative, as we proceed, will exhibit such of the public acts of Governor Chittenden as possess historical interest. No better connection than the present can perhaps be found to give a summary of his character. We quote from Thompson's History of Vermont. "Almost every age of the world has produced individuals, who seem to have been moulded by nature particularly for the exigencies of the times in which they lived. There have always been some master spirits, who were peculiarly fitted to control the agitated waters of public opinion, and either to soothe them into a calm, or else to mount upon the wind and direct the waves; and the results attained under their guidance have usually been happy or otherwise, according as the ruling motives of the leaders have been patriotic or selfish. These results, it is true, are materially affected by the amount of virtue and intelligence among the people; but virtue and intelligence do not, alone, fit an individual for becoming a popular and successful leader in troublesome times. There is necessary, in addition to these, a certain indescribable tact and native energy which few individuals have possessed, and which, perhaps, no one in our state has manifested in a more eminent degree than Governor Chittenden.

"He had not, indeed, enjoyed many of the advantages of education; but his want of learning was amply compensated by the possession of a strong and active mind, which at the time he emigrated to Vermont was matured by age, practised to business, and enriched by a careful observance of men and things. His knowledge was practical rather than theoretic. He was regular in his habits, plain and simple in his manners, averse to ostentation of equipage or dress; and he cared little for the luxuries, the blandishments, or the etiquette of refined society. In short, though he was destitute of many of the qualifications now deemed essential in a statesman, he possessed all that were necessary, and none that were superfluous, in the times in which he lived; and he was probably far better fitted to be the leader and governor of the independent, dauntless and hardy, but uncultivated settlers of Vermont, than would have been a man of more theoretic knowledge or polite accomplishments."

The very first meeting of the Vermont legislature was embarrassed by the presentation of a dilemma. The New Hampshire towns contiguous to

Vermont had not been unmindful of the proceedings of the new state, and having a community of feeling and interest with the people of this model commonwealth, they were desirous of a closer union. Accordingly, on March 12th, the first day of the assembling of the legislature, a petition was presented from sixteen towns in New Hampshire, praying to be admitted as members of the state of Vermont. The petition set forth that they, the said sixteen towns, "were not connected with any state with respect to their internal police." The argument by which they defended this assertion was, that the original grant of the province to John Mason was circumscribed by a line drawn at the distance of sixty miles from the sea, and not including the territory immediately adjoining the Connecticut River. These towns were, like Vermont west of the river, "New Hampshire grants," being annexed to that state solely by royal commissions, supplementary to the original charter. These commissions, they argued, could be of force no longer than while the authority of the crown subsisted; and as all royal authority was done away, the obligation which annexed them to the state of New Hampshire was done away with it. And they, therefore, reasoned that it belonged to the people to determine what state they would join, and what government they would be under. It did not perhaps occur to the friends of this measure that their argument proved too much, and that the same objections which they urged against the royal grants would operate with equal force against the original royal charter. But when the "wish is father to the thought," we cannot expect impartial reasoning or discriminating logic.

The disposal of the application was a sad puzzle to the neophytes in legislation. The representatives of the towns west of the mountains were decidedly opposed to the petitioners; and probably, could the question have been decided at once, the majority of the assembly would have voted to dismiss the petition. But the representatives of the towns on the Connecticut River, being allured by feelings of interest and neighbourhood to the petitioners, more than intimated that unless the New Hampshire towns were received, they would secede from Vermont, and join with the petitioners in the erection of a new state. Afraid of the responsibility of a decision, and unacquainted with their precise powers in such an unexpected position, the legislature adjourned on the 18th of March, to consult their constituents.

The advocates of the union of the new towns were indefatigable in their exertions to secure the members of the legislature and produce such an impression as they desired; and when the assembly met, by adjournment, on the 4th of June, it appeared that a majority of the members were in favour of the annexation. It was represented to the assembly that the inhabitants of these towns were unanimous in their desire to join Vermont, and that New Hampshire, as a state, would make no objection. Under these representations the assembly voted—thirty-seven to twelve—that the union should take place. And the assembly further resolved, that any other of the towns on the New Hampshire bank of the Connecticut River might come into Vermont, upon producing a vote of the inhabitants to that effect, or sending a representative. And having thus, with admirable indifference to what New Hampshire might say upon the subject, cut themselves off, with a provision to accommodate more deserting communities, the sixteen towns politely announced to the government of New Hampshire that they had shaken off her jurisdiction; and they requested that a division line might be established, and a friendly intercourse be still maintained between the severed members and New Hampshire.

As may readily be imagined, the New Hampshire legislature were not at all prepared to submit to a proceeding which would at once dismember their state, and establish a precedent which might lead to endless confusion. No landmarks and no boundaries would be safe under such latitudinarian construction. The legislature of New Hampshire authorized the president of the council of safety, Mesheck Weare, to correspond, under instructions, with Vermont, and with the delegates of the state in Congress. To the latter he wrote on the 19th of August, urging them to take advice and procure the interposition of Congress; intimating his apprehensions that this would be the only method in which the controversy could be settled without the effusion of blood, since all overtures of reconciliation made to the towns had been in vain.

To the governor of Vermont, Mr. Weare wrote, claiming the sixteen towns as part of New Hampshire. He based his claim on the known boundaries of the state before the Declaration of Independence; on their sending delegates to the provincial convention; on their petitions to the assembly for arms and ammunition; on their receiving commissions from the state government, and acting as a part of the state. He also announced that the minority in the sixteen towns had claimed that protection which the government was bound by every consideration to afford; and he urged Governor Chittenden to exert his influence with the assembly of Vermont to dissolve a connection which would endanger their peace, and probably their political existence. On the reception of this communication, Governor Chittenden convened the council, and the result of their deliberations was to despatch Colonel Ethan Allen to Philadelphia, to ascertain how the proceedings of Vermont were regarded by the members of Congress.

While in this dispute with New Hampshire, the government of Vermont was perplexed also with its New York difficulties. Governor Clinton was in correspondence with the adherents of New York in Vermont, and under his advice their proceedings began to take form and importance. In a letter of July 7th, to one of his friends, he said, "I would still, as on a former occasion, earnestly recommend a firm and prudent resistance to the draughting of men, raising of taxes, and the exercise of every act of government under the ideal Vermont state; and in towns where our friends are sufficiently powerful for the purpose, I would advise the entering into association for the mutual defence of their persons and estates against this usurpation." Governor Clinton also addressed Congress upon the same subject, urging that body to come to some decision. In this letter he reflected strongly upon Vermont for her proceedings, and predicted that without the interposition of Congress they must result in a civil war. And he declared that all the grievances of which Vermont complained, were from the former government of New York, and not from the present.

Governor Chittenden and his council had indeed a difficult course before them. In addition to these difficulties from without, and the partial disaffection within, which gave pretext to the New York pretensions, the spirit of the Green Mountain Boys made them not a little unmanageable. Having erected a state, and put the machinery of government into operation, they were not a little elated at their success, and at the appreciation of it which the New Hampshire towns showed in their desire for union. But the wings of the Vermont legislature were a little clipped by the report which they received from Philadelphia. Colonel Allen returned from his mission in October, and the assembly was summoned to act upon his communication.

The report which the messenger brought from Philadelphia was, the members of Congress were unanimously opposed to the dismemberment of New Hampshire; but that if proceedings in that regard were annulled, there would be nobody to oppose the admission of Vermont into the Union, except the representatives from New York. This understanding, of course, was informal, based on conversation with the members, and not on any action of Congress as a body. The subject was considered and debated several days, and was at length closed by three votes, indicating rather than affirming the opinion of the assembly.

At the first session of the legislature the state was divided into two counties. Bennington on the west, and Cumberland on the east of the mountains. On the question, "Shall the counties in this state remain as they were established in March last?" the vote was affirmative, thirty-five to twenty-six. The question, "Shall the towns on the east of the Connecticut River be included in the county of Cumberland?" the decision was in the negative: yeas twenty-eight, nays thirty-three. The question, "Shall said towns be erected into a county by themselves?" was negatived by the same vote. Discovering by these indications that the assembly hesitated to assume jurisdiction over the New Hampshire towns, the representatives from these towns withdrew, and were followed by the lieutenant-governor, two of the council, and fifteen members of the assembly from towns in Vermont proper. The number left was barely sufficient to form a quorum. The legislature finished its business, and adjourned to meet again in February, after in the mean while consulting their constituents. This mode of proceeding, to avoid responsibility, appears to have been quite a favourite course in the early days of the young state. It was certainly primitive and democratic.

The seceding members were not disposed to give up the matter, but entered a formal protest upon the journal of the assembly against its proceedings, and then went on to set up for themselves. They called a convention to assemble at Cornish, one of the sixteen towns, on the 9th of December, the understood object of which was to establish a new government, the centre of which should be the Connecticut River. Only eight towns on the west of the river were represented, and these did not enter very heartily into the proceedings, some of them declining to take any part. This convention proposed to New Hampshire to agree upon a division line—to submit the line to Congress, or to refer it to arbitration. Or, if none of these prepositions were acceptable, they declared that they were willing that the whole of the New Hampshire grants, now Vermont, should be re-annexed to New Hampshire, in accordance with the views of Governor Wentworth, who issued them.

The Green Mountain Boys opened their eyes. The whole animus of the movement was now apparent, the sixteen towns evidently having no other object than to form a government, the centre of which should be upon the Connecticut River. How this was to be done, whether by uniting a considerable part of New Hampshire with Vermont, or giving Vermont entire to New Hampshire, was a secondary consideration, provided only that the metropolis of the new state was in the valley of the Connecticut. Since the subject was brought home so directly to their own interest, they could perceive the injustice and impolicy of dismembering a state; and the legislature which met on the 11th of February barely gave itself time to organize before it dissolved the union with the New Hampshire towns.

But it is a great deal easier to make a false step than to retrieve it—to get into difficulty than to find the way out. Vermont formally notified New Hampshire of her decision, while at the same time the convention of seceders were operating upon the legislature of that state. The legislature of New Hampshire, acting upon the suggestion of some of her leading men, determined upon a summary settlement of the whole question. She resolved the *whole* of Vermont under her jurisdiction, in pursuance of the old Wentworth grants, and memoralized Congress accordingly. New York also put in her claim, and petitioned Congress for the whole territory in pursuance of the old royal decisions. The suspicion was not unreasonably entertained, that there was a purpose in these conflicting demands to divide the bone of contention between the two states, and settle the dispute by giving half of Vermont to each.

A new claimant now appeared, as if the matter were not already sufficiently complicated. Massachusetts demanded a share of the contested territory, and made a very plausible argument. New Hampshire had belonged to the jurisdiction of New York and Massachusetts, and the precise bounds between these two states were not yet determined. Whichever of the two contending states should acquire the disputed territory, Massachusetts would come in upon it like an encumbrance upon a contested estate. It is, however, a matter of doubt whether the motives of Massachusetts were really to assert a claim, or to postpone the absorption of the little state which was so gallantly contending with her powerful neighbours. Whatever might have been the intention, the effect was to save Vermont from being summarily divided.

CHAPTER XII.

Trouble with the adherents of New York in Vermont — Contrast between the New York and Vermont claimants — Principles involved in the dispute — Vermont Congregationalists — Wallumschaick — Tenure of Rev. Godfrey Dellius — Convention of "Yorkers" at Brattleboro — Petition to the governor of New York — Military organization — The New York officers captured by Ethan Allen — Appeals to Congress — Commissioners appointed by Congress — New York and New Hampshire authorize Congress to adjudicate between them — Massachusetts declines — Vermont makes an appeal to the world — Extracts from that document — Congress censures Vermont by resolution — Governor Chittenden's reply — Sagacity of Vermont statesmen — Agents from Vermont sent to observe the proceedings of Congress — Their withdrawal and protest — Indefinite postponement of the matter by Congress — Indian forays — False alarm.

THE condition of the little state of Vermont was now more perplexing than ever. Hitherto, while demonstrations had been made against her from without, there had been a majority within in favour of her independence, sufficient to overawe or silence the minority who supported the claims of New York. But now, acting upon the suggestions of Governor Clinton, and in keeping with the spirit and temper of the times, when every thing was determined by conventions and associations, the "Yorkers," as the adherents of that interest were termed, began to form themselves into organized bodies, to resist the authority of the "pretended state." The friends of the New York claims met in Brattleboro, on the 4th of May, 1779. The removal of foreign invasion from the vicinity of Vermont, by the capture of Burgoyne, appears to have given the disputants leisure to reimbark in their old disputes with increased zeal and acrimony.

There was something besides mere proprietorship in land which imbittered the contest. The actual settlers in Vermont were men who had made comparatively small purchases, and improved them by the labour of their own hands, and the joint assistance of their families. They had entered upon the work poor in money, but rich in resolution; in many cases bringing nothing with them except what could be transported on horseback. Others chose winter for their journey, and drew their little household gear on hand-sleds; and sometimes the mothers, if infirm, and the children, were drawn to the place of their future habitation by their husbands and brothers. And other families carried all their possessions in packs upon their shoulders. Thus, says a late writer, Mr. De Puy, would a single family move into a township, and reside months without seeing any other human being. Mr. Amos Cutler, the first settler in the town of Brandon, spent an entire winter without seeing any other person; and Mr. Abyah Wheelock, an early pioneer of Calais, after a flourishing town had grown up around him, would allude pleasantly to the hermit life he had formerly endured, by asserting that there had been a time when he was the most respectable man in the town! The wife of Thomas Whitmore, the earliest settler in Marlborough, spent the most of one winter alone, her husband being absent on business. This lady lived to the advanced age of eighty-seven years, and saw a flourishing state grow up where a few scattered families resided when she entered the territory.

Being chiefly emigrants from Connecticut and Massachusetts, the Vermont settlers carried with them the practically democratic notions of those commonwealths. In some respects they were even in advance of their New England compatriots, giving the first lesson to New England of true religious liberty. The first church organized on the grants was at Bennington, in 1762; and while the members still denominated themselves Congregationalists, and adopted the Cambridge "platform," or confession of faith and rules of discipline, they omitted such parts as united the secular and ecclesiastical powers. The aid of the civil magistrates in enforcing the support of the ministry, and their power over the church in other respects, was never admitted in Vermont.

To men who held such sentiments, the semi-feudal tenure of the New York grants was particularly odious. They wished a state of freeholders, and not of tenants. They desired no class of "patroons" in feudal lordship over leaseholders. It is curious to observe how history may be traced in trifling circumstances. Almost the only memorial of the attempted engraftment of the feudal tenure upon Vermont, is in the name of the little stream called the Walloomschaick, a branch of the Hoosac River. A Dutch gentleman named Wallum purchased Bennington of the governor of New York, before the issue of the New Hampshire grants. Thence the tract was called Wallumschaick, afterward changed to its present orthography—schaick meaning scrip or patent. The first disputes with the settlers were upon this patent.

Another New York grant, dated as far back as 1696, when Governor Fletcher, of New York, conferred upon Godfrey Dellius, minister of the Dutch church in Albany, eight hundred and forty square miles of the present territory of Vermont, the condition of the conveyance being, "He Yielding, Rendering and Paying therefore Yearly and every Year unto Us, our Heirs and Successors on the Feast Day of the Annunciation of our Blessed Virgin Mary at our City of New Yorke the Annual Rente of one Raccoon Skinne, in liew and stead of all other Rents, Services, Dues, Dutyes and demands whatsoever for the said Tract of Land and Islands and Premises." For the same tract Dellius, who seemed disposed "to make assurance doubly sure," and get the full value of raccoon skins, obtained a grant from the Mohawk Indians. But a succeeding governor of New York recommended the legislature to annul the grants, which was done accordingly. The same legislature suspended Dellius from the ministry for "deluding the Mohawk Indians, and illegal and surreptitious obtaining of said grants." Yet Dellius transferred his claim to Rev. John Lydius, his successor. The heirs of Lydius sold under that title, and the government of New York chose to recognise the claim during the disputes with Vermont. Ethan Allen and the Green Mountain Boys summarily dispossessed the settlers who came upon their soil under such a pretext. They were reinstated and re-ejected, and this "illegal and surreptitious deluding" was the basis of much trouble to the Green Mountain Boys. The holders under New York of these and similar titles were men of large fortunes, and often obtained their large grants upon such terms of favouritism that they could afford easy conditions to those who would settle under them. It is easy to see, as we have already observed, that the sturdy and practical republicans of Vermont found principle as well as mere interest involved in these disputes.

But the New York party were pertinacious. They met, as we have stated, at Brattleboro, and drew up a petition to the governor of New York, in which they related their grievances, and the proceedings which were in progress to confiscate their property, and entreated his excellency to "take immediate measures for protecting the loyal subjects of that part of the state, and for convincing Congress of the impropriety of delaying a decision in a matter which so nearly concerned the peace, welfare, and lives of so many of their firm adherents." Possibly the fellow-feeling of large landholders in New York, who had similar tenures to the disputed ones in Vermont, created an interest in their favour. The petition was replied to by the governor of New York, with assurance of protection, and the recommendation that the authority of Vermont should not be submitted to, except in cases where the alternative was absolute ruin.

The petitioners took another step in their plans of resistance. They formed a military association, and representing that they could form a regiment of five hundred men, obtained the necessary commissions from New York for their officers, and begged, in addition, the aid of the militia of Albany county. The resistance to this movement by Vermont was prompt. Colonel Ethan Allen had, upon his return, been invested with the command of the Vermont militia, and Governor Chittenden directed him to call out a force and meet this difficulty. Colonel Allen marched as directed, and made prisoners of the New York colonel and some other officers. The governor of New York was instantly appealed to, in behalf of his officers held in duress by the Green Mountain Boys. Governor Clinton, in answer to a former communication, had assured the adherents of New York, in Vermont, that if any attempt was made to reduce them by force of arms, he would instantly issue his orders to the militia, "who were properly equipped, and who would instantly be led against the enemies of the state, wherever they might happen to be." Probably he did not, when he wrote this promise, conceive of the possibility of a case arising under which it might be claimed. At any rate wiser counsels prevailed than the opposition of force by force. Governor Clinton contented himself with an appeal to Congress, which body he had already addressed upon the same subject within a month. In the former letter he adverted to the necessity which was impending that he should call out an armed body. He intimated the possible consequences of such a proceeding, but said that justice, the faith of government, and the peace and safety of society would not permit New York to remain passive while such acts of violence were committed on her citizens.

In answer to this letter, Congress, by a resolution of June 1st, appointed a committee of their body to repair to the district known as the New Hampshire grants, and inquire of the inhabitants why they refused to continue citizens of

93

the respective states claiming jurisdiction over them. The committee were instructed to take all prudent measures to restore quiet, and prevent animosities and divisions so prejudicial to the United States. Governor Clinton's second letter, advising Congress of the actual appeal to arms, arrived before the above-named committee had departed on their mission. Congress passed a second resolution, June 16th, in which they declared that the officers captured by Vermont ought immediately to be liberated, and instructed their committee to investigate this proceeding also.

Five commissioners were appointed to repair to Vermont; two only of whom attended. They made many inquiries, held many conferences with gentlemen of all parties, and effected nothing. Exasperation had gone too far to admit of compromise or reconciliation. Four parties claimed jurisdiction— New York, New Hampshire, Massachusetts, and Vermont; and it was not in the power of a body like Congress, which had really no authority, except by concession, to adjudicate between them. The difficulty was perceived, and in order to remove it, Congress earnestly recommended New Hampshire, Massachusetts, and New York, to *authorize* the national Congress to settle the dispute for them relative to *their* boundaries. Poor little Vermont was entirely ignored in this matter, Congress advising those persons who denied the territorial claims of the above-named states to abstain from the attempt to exercise authority over those who admitted their jurisdiction. At the same time the said states were requested to abstain from executing their laws over those who "have assumed a separate jurisdiction, which they call the state of Vermont."

Nothing could be better for New York and New Hampshire than this proposal. Vermont was unrepresented in Congress, and unacknowledged; and her neighbours had only to divide her territory between them, and thus settle the dispute by extinguishing the new government. Fortunately for the gallant little state, she had a fast friend in Massachusetts, and the sage counsellors of that commonwealth effectually barred proceedings, by neglecting or refusing to authorize Congress to act on the Massachusetts claim. The uncertainty and doubt which had hung over the settlements on the grants were as great and troublesome as ever. Indeed, if there was any change it was to the disadvantage of Vermont, since the proceedings of Congress evinced a willingness to sacrifice Vermont, rather than cause a rupture with the two states which claimed her soil, or with either of them. In this dilemma Vermont had no choice but to defend the position she had assumed; since the recognition of four separate jurisdictions was incompatible with any condition of society. Moreover, New York increased and aggravated the difficulty by granting commissions to her adherents in the several towns, encouraging spies, denying the acts of the state and the titles of the settlers to their lands.

In order to keep their true position before the world, the governor and council of Vermont published an appeal on the 10th of December, 1779, in reference to the foregoing resolutions of Congress. It was drawn up by Stephen R. Bradley, Esq., and while as firm in tone as the Green Mountain Boys' manifestoes, it is correct and chaste in language. We subjoin a few paragraphs. The appeal, in behalf of the inhabitants of Vermont, declared "that they could not hold themselves bounden, in the sight of God or man, to submit to the execution of a plan which they had reason to believe was commenced by neighbouring states: That the liberties and privileges of the state of Vermont by said resolutions are to be suspended upon the arbitrement and final disposition of Congress, when, in their opinion, they were things too sacred ever to be arbitrated upon at all, and what they were bound to defend at every risk: That the Congress of the United States had no right to intermeddle in the internal police and government of Vermont: That the state existed, independent of any of the thirteen United States, and was not accountable to them, or to their representatives for liberty, the gift of the beneficent Creator: That the state of Vermont was not represented in Congress, and could not submit to resolutions passed without their consent, or even knowledge, and which put every thing that was valuable to them at stake: That there appeared a manifest irregularity, not to say predetermination, that Congress should request of their constituents power to judge and determine in the cause, and never ask of thousands whose all was at stake: They also declared that they were, and ever had been ready to hear their proportion of the burden and expense of the war with Great Britain, from its first commencement, whenever they were admitted into the Union with the other states: But they were not so lost to all sense and honour, that after four years' war with Great Britain, in which they had expended so much blood and treasure, that they should now give up all worth fighting for, the

95

right of making their own laws and choosing their own form of government, to the arbitration of any man or body of men under Heaven."

Congress had proposed to take up the matter in dispute, on the 1st of February, 1780. But the subject was not reached in that body until the 2d of June. On that day it was resolved that the proceedings of the people of the New Hampshire grants were highly unwarrantable, and subversive of the peace and welfare of the United States; and that they be strictly required to forbear from any acts of authority, civil or military, over those of the people who professed allegiance to other states. By resolution on a subsequent day, the matter was deferred until September.

When these resolves reached Vermont, Governor Chittenden, by advice of his council, replied, that "however Congress might view these resolutions, they were considered by the people of Vermont as being in their nature subversive of the natural right which they had to liberty and independence, as well as incompatible with the principles on which Congress grounded their own right to independence, and had a natural and direct tendency to endanger the liberties of America: That Vermont, being a free and independent state, had denied the authority of Congress to judge of their jurisdiction; *that as they were not included in the thirteen United States, if necessitated to it, they were at liberty to offer or accept terms of cessation of hostility with Great Britain, without the approbation of any other man or body of men;* for, on proviso that neither Congress, nor the legislatures of those states which they represent, will support Vermont in her independence, but devote her to the usurped government of any other power, she had not the most distant motive to continue hostilities with Great Britain, and maintain an important frontier for the United States, and for no other reward than the ungrateful one of being enslaved by them; but notwithstanding the usurpation and injustice of neighbouring governments toward Vermont, and the late resolutions of Congress, yet, from a principle of virtue, and close attachment to the cause of liberty, as well as from a thorough examination of their own policy, they were induced once more to offer union with the United States of America, of which Congress were the legal representative body."

When we consider the difficult position of Vermont, and the menaces which overhung her in so many directions, we cannot but admire the sagacity of her statesmen. While her very existence as a state was denied, and she had no representation in Congress, she was compelled to defend herself both against the manifest influence of that body and against the machinations of her powerful neighbours. But the part which Congress had to perform was at least as difficult; and while contemporaries complained of the inaction of the representatives of the confederated states, we can now readily perceive that their true wisdom was to temporize. In September, 1780, the vexed question of jurisdiction came up again. Although Vermont had protested against the authority of Congress to legislate away her existence, and adjudicate upon her jurisdiction while she had no representatives in that body, still, as a matter of prudence, she sent Ira Allen and Stephen R. Bradley as her agents to watch the proceedings. These agents were admitted to a seat in the house, but not to a voice or a vote. They remained until they perceived, by the course of proceedings, that the contest was regarded as one between New York and New Hampshire, without any recognition of the existence of Vermont as a separate territory. Indignant at such proceedings, but without power to interrupt them, the agents refused to sit as tame witnesses of the disfranchisement of the commonwealth they represented, and withdrew themselves from the sessions of Congress.

They put in, however, as the agents of Vermont, a protest, similar in general tone and expression to the appeals and letters of the Vermont authorities, but making this strong point on the question before Congress: If the dispute is between the states claiming on the one part, and Vermont on the other, whether Vermont has a *right* to the legislative power which she possesses *in fact*, then Vermont should be heard or considered as to the question of *right*. If that right be disproved, the assumed authority must go with it; but to deny the jurisdiction in the first place is to deny that there are any parties to the dispute. The remonstrants declared that they could no longer sit as idle spectators, without betraying the trust reposed in them, and doing violence to their own feelings; that, by the mode of trial adopted, Vermont could have no hearing without denying her own existence, and that they would not take upon themselves such humility and self-abasement as to lose their political life in order to find it. They expressed the willingness of Vermont to submit the dispute to the mediation and settlement of independent states; they freely consented that Congress should interpose to prevent the effusion of blood, but denied the right of that body to sit as a court of judicature and decide the controversy by virtue of authority given to it by one party only in the dispute. After hearing New Hampshire and New York, and receiving the protest of Vermont, Congress indefinitely postponed the whole subject.

While Vermont was thus struggling with her countrymen for political existence, and the recognition of her rights, the enemy were making an incursion into her territories. A party of three hundred Indians, commanded by a British officer, destroyed the settlement of Royalton, carrying away twenty-five prisoners, and killing four of the inhabitants. About twenty houses were burned, and as many barns. Cattle and sheep were slaughtered, and after a foray of several hours they were enabled to decamp unharmed, by threatening the lives of their prisoners if pursued. All the prisoners taken, except one who died in captivity, returned the next summer to their friends.

Amid the alarms of the period there occurred one which furnished the subject of border mirth for many years. A party of settlers while surveying, undertook to imitate the war-whoop, and succeeded so well that the fright ran from settlement to settlement, till the originators of it were scared among the rest at the fright which their own folly had produced. The militia were ordered out—people ran from their dwellings in a panic, teams were left harnessed in the fields, and bread to burn in the ovens. Night brought a snow storm, and new horrors, for the blaze of burning dwellings seemed to light up the heavens. A few hours dispelled the illusion. The fires were found to be brush heaps, and the whole affair a false alarm. During the remainder of the war there were occasional isolated cases of murder by the Indians; but for reasons which will shortly appear in our narrative, the British kept their savage allies quiet, and the land had rest.

CHAPTER XIII.

Vermont assumes the aggressive — Convention of New Hampshire towns — Second union with Vermont — Union of New York towns with Vermont — Causes which led to this state of things — British overtures to Ethan Allen — Cessation of hostilities to exchange prisoners — Commissioners appointed to arrange the terms — Other business before the commissioners — Ethan Allen encloses the British letters to Congress — Extracts from his letter to that body — Renewal of the negotiations for "exchange of prisoners" — Colonel Ira Allen's three weeks in Canada — Interesting documents — British instructions — Green Mountain diplomacy — Ira Allen's commission — His report to the Vermont assembly — Secret correspondence — Lord Germain's letter to Clinton — Impatience of the British agents — The constitution of the new royal province agreed upon by Colonel Allen and Major Fay — The British demand the new government of Vermont should be proclaimed — Colonel Allen assents on condition of some further delay — The British appear on Lake Champlain provided with proclamations — They send an apology for killing an American soldier — Suspense and curiosity of the American soldiers and citizens — Commotion in Governor Chittenden's office — A dilemma — Skilful escape — Surrender of Cornwallis — Retirement of the British into Canada.

VERMONT, having acted hitherto upon the defensive, with the exception of the very short time during which the sixteen New Hampshire towns were admitted into union with her; and having dissolved that union under an implied promise which had not been kept, and finding her prospect of admission into the confederacy still distant, determined to take an aggressive attitude. The course which New York and New Hampshire had pursued, wounded the pride of the stormy young republic, and she was desirous to pursue such a course as should compel the justice for which she had pleaded in vain.

The opportunity for such a change of policy presented itself early in 1781. The towns in New Hampshire adjoining the Connecticut River were still uneasy and unsettled. Many of the leading citizens cherished their old desire for change. The most feasible mode appeared to be the union of Vermont to

New Hampshire, and with this view a convention was called at Charleston, and circulars were sent to the towns in western New Hampshire inviting them to send delegates. They met accordingly, on the 16th of January, but the movers of the measure were not a little astonished to find a majority of the convention in favour of joining Vermont again, instead of annexing Vermont to New Hampshire. We are without the evidences of any such fact, but it would not seem unlikely that the busy Vermonters had made some exertion among their New Hampshire friends to bring about a result so unlooked for. However that may have been, the majority, and a large one, being in favour of the measure, a committee was chosen to confer with the assembly of the state of Vermont upon the subject.

Accordingly, in the month following, the assembly of Vermont were officially informed of what they were well apprized before, to wit: That the convention of the New Hampshire towns was desirous of being united with Vermont, in one separate independent government, upon such principles as should be mutually thought the most equitable and beneficial to the state. This application was referred to the committee, who reported on the 14th of February, that: In order to quiet the present disturbances on the two sides of the Connecticut River, and the better to enable the inhabitants to defend their frontier, the legislature of this state do lay a jurisdictional claim to all the lands east of Connecticut River, north of Massachusetts, west of Mason's Line, and south of latitude 45°, but that they will not, for the time being, exercise jurisdiction. This resolution passed.

At the same session, and on the same day, Vermont generously took a part of New York under her protection. A number of the inhabitants in the adjacent parts of New York, being that tract of country between Massachusetts and the Hudson River, prayed that Vermont would defend them against the enemy in Canada, and receive them into union with her. The legislature of Vermont accordingly passed a resolution laying claim to the district in question, taking in also all the land east of a line from the head of the Hudson to latitude 45°—a pretty generous appropriation, as it included Lake Champlain entire, and much territory west of that lake. There was the same proviso about jurisdiction in this resolve as in the resolution to divide New Hampshire.

Without an understanding of all the influences in operation, these paper enlargements of the state of Vermont may appear to the reader at the present day mere legislative bravado. But it was well understood that the British ministers and officers had high hopes of Vermont from the manner in which that sturdy little state had been treated by her more powerful neighbours, and by Congress. And so bitter had been the contest, and so ominous though unintelligible the threats of the indignant Vermont officers, that it was generally believed in the other states her leading men would incline to a union with Canada, if no other alternative existed but submission to New York. This belief brought whatever British leaven existed in New York and New Hampshire to favour the proposed union. This also operated to prevent Congress from proceeding to decide the controversy between New York and New Hampshire. Convenient questions of the power of the federal delegates to form a new state were raised, and thus they avoided all three horns of the dilemma, for to disoblige either of the parties in the contest would have been alike dangerous. And while the leading men of Vermont never for an instant faltered in their attachment to the cause of freedom, they were too politic to throw away any advantage which lay in their road. Vermont had now a nominal territory which was quite large enough, and she proceeded to dispose of lands without any heed to the grants which had been made by New York.

A year before the date of the proceedings which we have just narrated, in April, 1780, Colonel Ethan Allen had received overtures from the British authorities in Canada, for a union of Vermont with Canada. In the street at Arlington, Colonel Allen was accosted by a man in the disguise of an American farmer, who afterward proved to be a British soldier. This man was the bearer of a letter which Allen read, and dismissed the messenger. The contents of the letter were immediately laid before some confidential friends, including Governor Chittenden, and the result of their deliberations was that the matter should be passed over in silence, and no answer returned. The letter set forth the grounds upon which it was written, thus: "I have often been informed that you and most of the inhabitants of Vermont are opposed to the wild and chimerical scheme of the Americans in attempting to separate from Great Britain, and establish an independent government of their own, and that you would willingly assist in uniting America to Great Britain, and in restoring that happy constitution so wantonly and unadvisedly destroyed. If I have been rightly informed, and these should be your sentiments and inclination, I beg that you will communicate to me without reserve, whatever proposals you would wish to make to the commander-in-chief; and I hereby promise that I will faithfully lay them before him, according to your directions, and flatter myself that I can do so with as good effect as any person whatever. I can make no proposals to you until I know your sentiments; but think, upon your taking an active part and embodying the inhabitants of Vermont under the crown of England, you may obtain a separate government under the king and constitution of England, to act as the commander-in-chief shall direct, and the men, formed into regiments under such officers as you shall recommend, be on the same footing as all the provincial corps are. If you should think proper to send a friend of your own here, with proposals to the general, he shall be protected and well treated here, and allowed to return whenever he pleases." This letter was dated at New York, then in the occupation of the British, and signed by Colonel Beverly Robinson. But the movement was made under instructions from the British cabinet, as subsequently appeared.

While these overtures were making to Colonel Allen from the direction of New York, similar proposals were received from Canada. The British cabinet had high hopes to effect by negotiation and purchase, what they had failed to do by invasion. The connection of New York and Canada, by way of the Hudson and Lake Champlain, which Burgoyne had not accomplished, was to be effected by the corruption of the Green Mountain Boys. The attempted treachery of Arnold was no doubt a part of the same plot. And in this aspect of the case we perceive why reasons of state and stern necessity demanded the execution of the unfortunate Andre. It was more than suspected, even at this time, that the enemy were at work by emissaries; and it was the rigid demand of war that such messengers should be summarily dealt with.

Governor Chittenden, in July, 1780, sent a flag into Canada requesting the release or exchange of certain prisoners who had been carried into Canada. In the fall of the same year the British came up Lake Champlain in great force, and despatched a flag with a very favourable reply to Governor Chittenden's request, and a proposition for the cessation of hostilities between the Vermont and the British forces during the negotiation of the exchange. Colonel Ethan Allen, commanding the Vermont militia, consented to the cessation, provided

102

the adjacent frontier of New York should be included. The reader will not fail to perceive in this sagacious conduct of Colonel Allen, the origin, in part at least, of the petition soon after presented by the inhabitants of the New York towns to be admitted into Vermont. The affairs of that state were in reality managed by about a dozen of the most shrewd and farseeing men in the world, and they played their difficult role, in part openly and in part secretly, in a manner which deserves far more attention than it has usually received from the annalist.

Colonel Ira Allen and Major Joseph Fay were appointed commissioners on the part of Vermont to meet the British agents, and arrange the terms of the exchange of prisoners. If they were not before apprized of the motives of the British commander for his extraordinary condescension and friendliness, their eyes were now opened. There was a much deeper purpose than the exchange of prisoners in the movements of the British commander. The same proposals were verbally made to the Vermont commissioners, from the Canadian officers, as had been made by letter from New York to Ethan Allen. The commissioners received the proposals with great good humour, and so evaded any direct answer, though still holding out hopes and promises, that they procured a continued cessation of hostilities, and the enemy retired to Canada without having injured the people of Vermont in any particular, or made any hostile movements.

Immediately upon these events followed the annexation measures which we have already related. While the assembly were legislating, the secret rulers of Vermont were busy with their correspondence. Ethan Allen, in February, received another letter from Colonel Robinson, enclosing a copy of the first, which he supposed had miscarried. In his second letter, Colonel Robinson spoke with increased confidence, based on "frequent accounts received for three months past." No doubt these accounts were the favourable reports which the Canada negotiators had furnished to the commander in New York. So confident was he of the defection of Vermont from the republican cause, that he desired information in what manner the people of Vermont could be most serviceable to the British government, whether by acting with the northern army or joining an army from New York.

Ethan Allen returned no answer to either of these letters, but in March enclosed them in a letter to Congress, informing that body of all the circumstances which had attended the business. We extract from the letter the following passage: "I am confident that Congress will not dispute my sincere attachment to the cause of my country, though I do not hesitate to say I am fully grounded in opinion that Vermont has an indubitable right to agree on terms of a cessation of hostilities with Great Britain, provided the United States persist in rejecting her application for a union with them. For Vermont would be of all people most miserable, were she obliged to defend the independence of the united claiming States, and they be, at the same time, at full liberty to overturn and ruin the independence of Vermont. When Congress considers the circumstances of this state, they will, I am persuaded, be more surprised that I have transmitted them the enclosed letters than that I have kept them in custody so long; for I am as resolutely determined to defend the independence of Vermont as Congress is that of the United States; and rather than fail, I will retire with the hardy Green Mountain Boys into the desolate caverns of the mountains, and wage war with human nature at large."

In the spring of 1781 the British authorities in Canada renewed their overtures. Colonel Ira Allen was sent to the British quarters upon the old pretext—an exchange of prisoners. He soon found himself engaged in the unfinished business of last year, the restoration of Vermont to the British crown. He remained in Canada nearly three weeks, and was engaged every day in a skilful contest of diplomacy with the agent of General Haldiman. The documents in relation to this business, preserved by Hon. Henry Stevens of Vermont, and recently first published in Du Pay's "Ethan Allen," present the subject in a clearer light than it ever has been shown before. They consist of the instructions of General Haldiman to his agent, that agent's report of his proceedings, and two formal endorsements of the doings of the Vermont agents by Governor Chittenden and his council. The instructions of Haldiman make the same promises that we have already noticed, with definite offers of the command of battalions, and the rank of lieutenant-colonel to Ethan Allen and Governor Chittenden. The most remarkable feature in the document is the profound commiseration for the wrongs of Vermont at the hands of her sister states and Congress, which General Haldiman professed to entertain. "I agree," he says, "that this negotiation shall cease, and any steps that led to it be forgotten, provided the Congress shall grant the state of Vermont a seat in their assembly, and acknowledge its independency. I trust that time and other methods will bring about a reconciliation and a return to their allegiance," &c. &c.

Whatever General Haldiman may have intended in the above—whether a covert threat, to induce Vermont to cease her efforts to be admitted into the American Union, or a show of greater magnanimity from an enemy than Vermont received from her countrymen, British diplomacy was lost upon Ira Allen. That shrewd, and, we suspect, not overscrupulous negotiator, managed to befog his antagonist through the whole three weeks, exciting hopes which were untangible when it was sought to reduce them to terms, and adhering to verbal communications entirely. Nothing but the great importance of securing Vermont could have induced the British officer thus to parley. The letter of Ethan Allen to Congress, which we have referred to above, was shown by Ira Allen to the British officer, with the greatest show of frankness, as was also the circular letter of the governor of Vermont to the other states, begging for assistance against the threatened British invasion, and the British officer was assured that these steps were only taken by Ethan Allen and Governor Chittenden for their own personal safety. We know not whether most to wonder at the effrontery of the one or the credulity of the other party.

We present one of the endorsements of Ira Allen's proceedings entire, as it places the attitude in which the Vermont statesmen stood distinctly before the reader: "Whereas this State is not in union with the United States, altho' often Requested, &c. This the British Power are acquainted with, and are endeavouring to take the advantage of these disputes Thereby to court a connection with this State on the Principle of Establishing it a British Province—from various accounts we are well assured that the British have a force in Canada larger than this State can at present raise and support in the field; and this State having no assurance of any assistance from any or either of the United States, however hard the British forces may crowd on this state from the Province of Quebeck, by the advantage of the waters of Lake Champlain, &c. Altho' several Expresses have been sent by the Gov'r of this State, to several of the respective Gov'rs of the United States, with the most urgent requests to know whether any assistance would be afforded in such case, and no official answer has been made by either of them.

"Wherefore, we, the subscribers, do fully approbate Col. Ira Allen sending a Letter dated Sunderland, July 10th, 1781, and directed to General

Haldimand, and another Letter to Captain Justice Sherwood, Purporting an Intention of this State's becoming a British Province, &c. This we consider as a Political Procedure to prevent the British forces invading this State; and being a necessary step to Preserve this State from Ruin, when we have too much reason to apprehend that this has been the wishes of some of our assuming neighbours. In the mean time, to strengthen this State against any insult, until this State receive better treatment from the United States, or obtain a seat in Congress." This document is dated July 10th, 1781, and signed by Governor Chittenden and five others.

These proceedings could not take place without exciting suspicions that something more was done in a seventeen days' conference than to arrange about the exchange of prisoners. And when it was understood that Colonel Ira Allen would report to the Vermont assembly, there was a large attendance of interested spectators—not only citizens of Vermont, but Whigs from other states jealous of treasonable practices, and agents from Canada, watching for the royal interest. The council met the assembly in joint committee. Governor Chittenden arose and stated that Colonel Allen had been sent to Canada to obtain the release of sundry persons belonging to Vermont, who were prisoners in the hands of the enemy, and that with much difficulty he had completed the business in behalf of Vermont, though no such exchange had taken place with the United States, or with any other individual state. He added, that Colonel Allen was present and could best give any further information, if desired.

The reader can scarcely forbear a smile at the governor's truly parental management, and his prudent reserve on doubtful topics. It is to our ears most primitive legislation; but the Vermont managers understood very well what they were doing. The Canadians, and the few others who were in the secret, must have been highly diverted. Colonel Allen followed, and endorsed the governor's statement, and concluded by stating that his papers had been left at home, but he would bring them the next day and submit them for inspection. The fact of an officer, with a report to make, leaving his documents at home, would appear rather preposterous if we were not in possession of some facts respecting other papers, which may throw some light on this omission. On the next day the papers were produced and examined, and found perfectly satisfactory. The negotiations about the armistice and the royal government had all been done verbally, and nothing, of course, appeared in the written report which could give a colour to the rumoured treason. Colonel Allen professed himself ready to answer any questions. The friends of the United States complimented Colonel Allen on his openness and candor, and the Canadians returned satisfied with his astuteness and caution.

While the little knot of diplomatists were thus parleying with the enemy, the great body of the Vermont people were inveterate in their hatred against the British and tories. Yet for nearly two years the Allens kept up their correspondence undetected, if not entirely unsuspected. On one occasion, Colonel Ira Allen met a party in Sunderland, who were preparing to pull down the house of a loyalist accused of too friendly feeling for the British. Allen prevailed on them to return home and relinquish their design. On the same spot, and on the same evening that he had coaxed these ardent whigs to disperse, Colonel Allen, by appointment, received a packet from a British messenger. But the difficult game could not be played too long, and our Vermont managers found themselves more than once nearly at their wit's end before they had done with it. Events seemed to hurry the drama to a denouement, and among these was a most inopportune publication in the Pennsylvania Packet.

A letter from Lord Germain, containing instructions for Sir Henry Clinton, commander of the British forces in America, was intercepted and published. The following paragraphs made quite a sensation in Congress and elsewhere: "The return of the people of Vermont to their allegiance, is an event of the utmost importance to the king's affairs; and at this time, if the French and Washington really meditate an irruption into Canada, may be considered as opposing an insurmountable bar to the attempt. General Haldimand, who has those people and give them support, will, I doubt not, push up a body of troops to act in conjunction with them, and secure all the avenues through their country into Canada; and, when the season admits, take possession of the upper parts of the Hudson and Connecticut Rivers, and cut off the communication between them and the Mohawk country. How far they may be able to extend themselves southward or eastward, must depend on the numbers and disposition of the inhabitants."

The British agents became impatient. This publicity would mar all, they thought, if the plan were not speedily matured. Ira Allen and Major Fay managed to amuse them, in September, with a discussion over the details of the plan of government for the new royal province of Vermont. The matter was considered, item by item; and when the Vermonters could no longer, like the wife of Ulysses, postpone their suitors by undoing and reweaving, they were forced to confess that the web was finished and ready for wear. Then the British agents insisted that Vermont should immediately declare herself a British province. The agents of Vermont declared (and this was undoubtedly the truth) that Vermont was not yet ripe for the change. But the only compromise they could obtain, was that the British commander should issue his proclamation declaring the state a British province, and confirming the plan of government agreed on, the proclamation to be made during the coming session of the legislature in October; and the legislature to accept its conditions, and carry it into effect.

This was a hard condition to agree to—but even the shrewdness of Ira Allen could devise no escape, and the conference closed with this understanding. October came, and with it the session of the Vermont legislature. General St. Leger ascended Lake Champlain with a powerful British army, and a bountiful provision of printed proclamations, and landed at Ticonderoga. We may well imagine that the Vermont negotiators were in no little perplexity, and an incident which occurred, revealed to them, on a small scale, what would probably be the great explosion when their proceedings came to light. The Vermont troops were posted at Castleton, to watch the enemy. Their military operations were, of course, a mere feint, the commanders, General Enos and Colonels Fletcher and Wallbridge, being now in the secret, while the subordinate officers and men knew nothing of what had been done and was impending.

Scouting parties were sent out to keep up appearances. One of these, commanded by Sergeant Tupper, met a British party, and both supposing that they were fighting fair, shots were exchanged. Sergeant Tupper was killed, and his men retreated. General St. Leger ordered Tupper's body to be honourably buried, and sent his clothing to General Enos, with an open letter, in which he expressed his regret at the death of the sergeant. This communication and clothing were publicly delivered to General Enos, and the whole American force was presently in a buzz of surprise, suspicion, and indignation at such a most unusual mission between belligerents,—and no wonder.

The American commanders instantly wrote letters, and despatched them by express to Governor Chittenden at Charleston. They either had no person fit to entrust with the secret, or forgot to apprize their messenger, Mr. Hathaway, of the true state of the case. He rushed over the country with the sealed letters, and an open mouth, circulating, as he went, the strange news that the British general had sent to his friends the clothing of an American soldier, killed in due course of war, with an apology for his death. Hathaway reached the governor's room with a crowd at his heels, anxious for enlightenment on so strange a piece of intelligence. On opening the letters they were found to contain matters which could not safely be made public.

While the letters were passing from hand to hand among those who were in the secret, Major Runnels, an officer in the Vermont militia, entered the room, and demanded of Colonel Allen, "*Why* General St. Leger should be sorry Tupper was killed?" Allen replied that *he* could not tell. Runnells repeated the question, the whole assembly being agape for the answer. Allen replied that "All good men were sorry when good men were killed, which might be the case with St. Leger." Highly indignant at this reply, Runnels again loudly demanded to know "What could possibly induce a British general to be sorry when his enemy was killed, and to send his clothes to his widow?" Allen now angrily requested Major Runnels "to go to his regiment; and, at the head of that, demand of St. Leger the reasons of his sorrows, and not be there asking impertinent questions, and eating up the country's provisions while the frontiers were invaded!"

Words followed words, increasing in anger, and Allen was not sorry to perceive that this by-play, which he skilfully kept up till Runnels left the room, was drawing attention from the letters. The dangerous documents were smuggled out, the Board of War (all in the secret) was convened, and while Hathaway detailed his news, the quick-witted managers, apt in emergency, wrote letters which could be published, and substituted them for the original. These were read before the council and assembly to quiet the people. Major Fay and Colonel Allen were at the same time busy preparing despatches for the British agents. In these letters they assured them that matters were going on favourably, but as a report was in circulation that Cornwallis had surrendered—which report was doubtless unfounded—they thought it expedient to delay the proclamation, until more favourable news should remove all doubt as to the ability of the British forces to sustain the new province.

But an express which reached the British camp at Ticonderoga immediately after this communication was received, put a new complexion on affairs. It brought a confirmation of the rumoured surrender. Either in pursuance of orders, or fearful of being surrounded and captured in the elation of the Americans at such intelligence, St. Leger instantly re-embarked his forces, and went back to Canada, and into winter quarters. Thus ended a second campaign, in which management had protected Vermont, and with Vermont the Union, against an enemy of from seven to ten thousand men, without even a skirmish.

Probably nobody in the United States felt more rejoiced at the fall of Cornwallis than our Vermont negotiators. It had relieved them from a strait in which their condition seemed one of inextricable embarrassment; and no doubt through the winter the Board of War of Vermont had many a hearty laugh at the baffled queries of the indignant Major Runnels.

CHAPTER XIV.

Action of Congress in relation to Vermont — Conditions proposed preliminary to her admission into the Union — Protest of Vermont against the action of Congress, and refusal of Vermont to comply — Message of General Washington to Governor Chittenden — The governor's reply — Threatened disturbances — Letter of General Washington to Governor Chittenden — Vermont recedes from her refusal — Congress fails to perform its conditional promises — Protest of the agents of Vermont — Indignation in Vermont at the evasive course of Congress — British overtures still continued — Remarks of Dr. Williams upon the Canadian correspondence — Disturbances in Windham county — Appeals to Congress — Resolutions of censure passed by that body — Vermont menaced by Congress — Spirited remonstrance of Vermont — Disturbances in Guilford — Martial law — Ethan Allen's proclamation — The "Yorkers" driven out — Death of Colonel Seth Warner — Remarks upon his life and character.

THE publication of the letter of Lord Germain to the British commander in New York, as it gave importance to rumors of danger which already prevailed, and demonstrated what Vermont could do, if she chose, quickened the apprehension of Congress as to the necessity of doing some thing in the case of Vermont. And just at this juncture three delegates arrived in Philadelphia, empowered to negotiate for the admission of Vermont into the Union, and to take their seats as her representatives, if admitted. Under the spur of the letter of Germain, and the tide of popular opinion which was now setting in favour of the admission of Vermont, a committee of five were appointed by Congress to confer with the delegates from Vermont. On the 18th of August a conference was had between the committee of Congress and the Vermont delegates; and on the 20th of the same month a resolution was passed by Congress, demanding, as an indispensable preliminary to the admission of Vermont, that she should retreat into her old limits, and dissolve the connection which she had just formed with the New Hampshire and the New York towns.

With this resolution both New York and Vermont were dissatisfied. The former state, by resolution of her legislature, protested against the action of Congress in the premises, and denied the authority of Congress to intermeddle with the former territorial jurisdiction of any state, or to form a new state by dismembering an old one. And Vermont, which now held her legislative session in Charleston, one of the New Hampshire towns, also denied the authority of Congress to prescribe her limits, and resolved to hold the articles of union between the different portions of the state inviolate. She, however, professed a willingness to refer the question of her boundaries to commissioners mutually chosen; or, if admitted into the confederacy, she would then submit all such disputes to Congress.

At the same time that the resolutions of Congress were transmitted to Vermont, General Washington sent a verbal message to Governor Chittenden, desiring to know what were the real designs, views, and intentions of the people of Vermont; whether they would be satisfied with the independence proposed by Congress, or had it seriously in contemplation to join the enemy and become a British province. The governor, in his reply, dated November 14th, 1781, was explicit, candid, and decisive. He said that there were no people on the continent more attached to the cause of America than the people of Vermont, but that they were fully determined not to be put under the government of New York; that they would oppose this by force of arms, and would join with the British in Canada rather than submit to that government. Governor Chittenden confidentially detailed to General Washington, in this letter, the transactions of the Vermont negotiators with the enemy, and assigned as a reason for this course that, "Vermont, driven to desperation by the injustice of those who should have been her friends, was obliged to adopt policy in the room of power." With regard to the recent resolutions of Congress, offering hope of admission into the confederacy, Governor Chittenden, in his letter, ascribed these measures, not to the influence of the friends of Vermont but to the power of the enemies of the country. "Lord George Germain's letter wrought on Congress, and procured that from them which the public virtue of the people could not obtain."

Meanwhile Vermont was in some difficulty with her new acquisitions. There were in the New Hampshire towns, and in the New York district which had been annexed to Vermont, many persons who objected to the union, and the governments of those two states were called upon to aid them in their resistance. Vermont imprisoned New Hampshire officers, and New Hampshire retaliated in kind. There was talk of an armed posse, but nothing serious grew out of this difficulty. During the winter of 1781-2, bodies of New York and Vermont militia were placed in a hostile attitude in the towns belonging to New York which had joined Vermont. Happily the good sense and moderation of the commanders prevented any actual collision; but the danger of violence produced an alarm which invoked the attention of General Washington. That true patriot exerted his powers of pacification, and wrote a letter to Governor Chittenden, from which we extract the following:—

"It is not my business, neither do I think it necessary now, to discuss the origin of the right of a number of the inhabitants to that tract of country formerly distinguished by the name of the New Hampshire grants, and now known by that of Vermont. I will take it for granted that their right was good, because Congress, by their resolve of the 7th of August imply it, and by that of the 20th are willing fully to confirm it, provided the new state is confined to certain prescribed bounds. It appears, therefore, to me, the dispute of boundary is the only one that exists, and that being removed, all other difficulties would be removed also, and the matter terminated to the satisfaction of all parties. You have nothing to do but withdraw your jurisdiction to the confines of your old limits, and obtain an acknowledgment of independence and sovereignty, under the resolve of the 20th of August, for so much territory as does not interfere with the ancient established bounds of New York, New Hampshire, and Massachusetts. In my private opinion, while it behooves the delegates to do ample justice to a body of people sufficiently respectable by their numbers, and entitled by other claims to be admitted into that confederation, it becomes them also to attend to the interests of their constituents, and see, that under the appearance of justice to one, they do not materially injure the rights of others. I am apt to think this is the prevailing opinion of Congress."

The weight of General Washington's character, and the affection with which he was regarded, produced their effect; and in February, 1782, the letter of the commander-in-chief of the now victorious American forces being laid before the Vermont assembly, that body receded from its new territorial claims, and complied with the preliminary required by Congress, as the basis of negotiations for her admission into the Union. But her former refusal was under consideration in Congress at the very moment when she was retracing that false step. Resolutions were reported of a more positive character than any which had hitherto passed. By these, in case of the refusal of Vermont to retire within her original limits, her territory was to be divided between New York and New Hampshire. These resolutions failed, however, to pass, and the Vermont delegates arrived with an official statement of the compliance of Vermont with the requisition of Congress. A committee of Congress reported that Vermont having complied with the resolution of the 20th of August, the conditional promise therein became absolute. The report closed with a resolution to admit the new state. But Congress refused to fix a day for its consideration, and the state of Vermont found itself still unacknowledged.

The delegates who had been sent from Vermont in the full faith that a few formalities only stood between them and their seats in Congress, on the 19th of April addressed a letter to the president of that body, and returned home. In that letter they represented that Vermont, in consequence of the faith pledged to that state, had in the most ample manner performed what was required. They expressed their disappointment at the unexpected delay. Vermont, they stated, was now reduced to a critical situation by casting off a considerable portion of her strength, being exposed to the main force of the enemy in Canada, and destitute of aid from the United States. They were urgent that delay might not deprive them of the benefit of this confederation, and requested that they should be officially apprized when their attendance would be necessary.

The people of Vermont were justly indignant that they were thus trifled with; and the opinion became general that the assembly had been duped by the finesse of Congress. The inhabitants of the state, both as individuals, and through their assembly, determined to trouble Congress no more with their claims to admission into the confederacy, but to adhere to the boundaries which they had originally fixed, and Congress had recognised. They would defend their own jurisdiction, and rely upon their own strength. Still, as a matter of prudence, and to put themselves in a correct attitude, they again appointed agents to arrange the admission of the state into the Union, and waited now for overtures.

The Revolutionary War virtually ceased with the surrender of Cornwallis in 1781. Perhaps the withdrawal of the outside pressure upon the Union made Congress negligent of the claims into notice of which they had been driven by foreign machinations. The British overtures to Vermont had, however, by no means ceased. During the winter of 1781-2 they were repeated, and through the whole of the year the correspondence was kept up, principally on the part of the British officers. Offers of commissions to different persons were distinctly made. In July, Colonel Ira Allen was sent into Canada to request the release of two officers belonging to Vermont. The officers were released, and Colonel Allen was hard-pressed to negotiate a secret treaty; and all the skill of the Vermont diplomatist was required to avoid compliance, and still procure a continuance of the armistice. This, however, he effected. We must do General Haldiman the credit to pronounce him a most humane man, nor can we deny him the quality of sincerity in his professions of friendship for the Vermont people, and in his desire to do them a benefit. The last letter from Canada was written in March, 1783, when rumours of the peace had reached that province, and in it the writer expresses a regret that the "happy moment" for a reconciliation "could not be recalled." Still, the writer promised, "should any thing favourable present"—that is, a chance to be included in Canada be discovered—"you may still depend on his excellency's utmost endeavours for your salvation." We will dismiss this part of the history of Vermont with the remarks of Dr. Williams, the early historian of that state.

"Thus terminated a correspondence which occasioned many and various conjectures at the time it was carried on. On the part of the British it consisted of constant attempts and endeavours to persuade the leading men of Vermont to renounce their allegiance to the states of America, and become a British province. On the part of the gentlemen of Vermont, the correspondence consisted of evasive, ambiguous general answers and proposals, calculated not to destroy the British hopes of seduction, but carefully avoiding any engagements or measures that could be construed to be the act of the government. And it had for its object a cessation of hostilities, at a time when the state of Vermont, deserted by the continent, and unable to defend herself, lay at the mercy of the enemy in Canada

"Eight persons only in Vermont were in the secret of this correspondence. Each of them was known to be among the most confirmed friends to the American cause. They had avowed their sentiments and embraced the cause of their country from the beginning of the American war. They had suffered severely, often borne arms, and done every thing in their power to defend the independence of the states. And, through the whole of this correspondence they gave the most decisive proofs that they could not be bought or bribed by any offers of wealth and honour. But so odious were the British proceedings and government, at that time, to the people of America, that it was with difficulty the people of Vermont could be kept quiet, under the idea of a correspondence carried on with the British, though known to be designed for their protection. Once or twice there were small insurrections to demand explanations; and nothing but the well-known and strong attachment of the gentlemen concerned to the independence of Vermont and of America could have preserved them from open violence and destruction."

Having thus disposed of the Canada entanglement, it remains that we state the conclusion of the New York difficulty. During the year 1782, a draught of militia was ordered by the assembly of Vermont. Certain persons in Windham county, denying the jurisdiction of Vermont, resisted, and being furnished with New York commissions, civil and military, undertook an organized resistance. The militia were called out by Governor Chittenden, the leaders of the sedition were captured, several were fined or imprisoned, and five of the most obnoxious banished. New York appealed to Congress; and that body passed resolutions of censure against Vermont, for having exercised authority over persons who professed allegiance to New York. Congress directed restitution to be made to those who had been fined and banished, and that they should be admitted to return without molestation. Effectual measures were threatened to *enforce* compliance—but it was easier to threaten than to perform.

The governor and council of Vermont immediately replied to these resolutions of Congress in a spirited remonstrance. In this document Congress was reminded of its engagements to Vermont still unfulfilled, and the remonstrants claimed that Vermont had as good a right to independence as Congress. They asserted that Vermont had as much authority to pass resolutions prescribing measures to Congress, as that body had to interfere between that state and criminals punished in due course of law. The remonstrants asserted that Congress was pursuing the same measures toward Vermont, which Britain had used against the American colonies, and which it had been judged necessary to oppose at every risk and hazard: That such proceedings tended to make the liberty and natural rights of mankind a mere bubble, and the sport of politicians: That it was of no importance to America to pull down arbitrary power in one form, that they might establish it in another: That the inhabitants of Vermont had lived in a state of independence from the first, and would not submit to be resolved out of it by the influence which New York, their old adversary, had in Congress: That they were in full possession of freedom, and would remain independent, notwithstanding all the power and artifice of New York: That they had no controversy with the United States, considered as a whole, but were at all times ready and able to vindicate their rights and liberties against the usurpations of the state of New York.

The changes and delays of Congress were well objected to in the remonstrance. "Congress has been so mutable in their resolutions respecting Vermont that it is impossible to know on what ground to find them, or what they design next. At one time they guarantee to New Hampshire and New York their lands within certain described limits, leaving a place for the existence of Vermont; the next thing Vermont hears from them is, they are within those limits controlling the internal government of the state. Again, they prescribe preliminaries of confederation, and when these are complied with on the part of the state they unreasonably procrastinate the ratification." Against the measures of Congress the remonstrants declared they would appeal to the justice of his excellency, General Washington. They recommended that the matter should be left to the states interested rather than that Congress should be embroiled with it: protested against a decision upon *ex parte* evidence, and renewed their request that Congress should fulfil its conditional promise of admission, now become absolute by the compliance of Vermont with their terms. The Vermont assembly, at its next session in February, 1783, endorsed the action of the governor and council. Congress took no further steps in the business, and Vermont was left undisturbed, so far as the action of the United States was concerned. The assembly went annually through the form of electing agents to attend to the formalities of admission, whenever they should be advised that Congress was prepared for them. The internal police and laws of the state were conducted, and its government administered, as if Vermont were not only independent, but the only independent state in the world.

The disaffected citizens of Vermont, in the interest of New York, commonly called "Yorkers," kept up their resistance. The county in which the Yorkers were most numerous was Windham, and Guilford in that county was the head-quarters of the opposition. A majority of the inhabitants, and the town was then the most populous in the state, were Yorkers; and they annually appointed committees "to prevent the constable from acting," or "to defend the town against the pretended state of Vermont." To ensure a majority, the Yorkers frequently summoned an armed force from the neighbouring towns to keep the "new state" voters from the polls. In Guilford and some other places there were separate town organizations. Social order was at an end, flagitious handbills stirred up discord, relatives and friends were arrayed against each other, and even physicians were not allowed to visit the sick without passes from the several committees. Every thing was in a state of frightful anarchy and confusion, and it became imperiously necessary that the government should enforce its laws and jurisdiction.

In the summer of 1783, Colonel Ethan Allen was directed to call out the militia to suppress the insurrection and disturbance in the county of Windham. Proceeding to Guilford with an armed posse of one hundred men, he issued there the following characteristic proclamation: "I, Ethan Allen, declare that unless the people of Guilford peaceably submit to the authority of Vermont, the town shall be made as desolate as were the cities of Sodom and Gomorrah." The Yorkers, in defiance of this proclamation, firing upon Allen and his men, were pursued, and all captured or dispersed. The prisoners were put under bonds for their good behaviour, and compelled to furnish supplies and quarters for their captors. The taxes were collected under martial law, the property of the New York partisans being summarily seized and sold for the benefit of the state. Martial law in the hands of Ethan Allen was a summary process.

During the following winter the disturbances were renewed. Armed parties of the "Yorkers" resisted; but after some wounds and bruises, the forced collection of taxes, whipping, fines, and the pillory, the malecontents ceased their resistance, and either took the oath of allegiance to Vermont, or left the state. Many of them settled on lands in New York, which the legislature of that state had granted for the benefit of such sufferers. From this period all armed resistance to Vermont ceased; and although New York did not immediately acknowledge the independence of the new state, she suffered her claims to remain in abeyance.

At the close of the year 1784 died Colonel Seth Warner. He was one of the master spirits among the Green Mountain Boys, and the first who received a commission from the United States. He was very active and useful to the cause, an intrepid soldier and a good officer. Colonel Warner had all the elements of success as a popular leader. In person he was commanding, in manners winning, and in exigencies prompt and active. He possessed those useful qualities which eminently fit a man for backwoods life. He was a skilful botanist, ready with simple remedies to be the physician and surgeon, as well as the commander of his men. He was a good huntsman, and his unerring aim and physical hardihood commanded respect where such properties were indispensable. He was in constant service during the war, and possessed in a high degree the confidence of General Washington, by whom he was employed in many difficult and responsible duties. His death, in his forty-second year, was the result of disease produced by the fatigues he had undergone. A native of Connecticut, he returned to that state to die, and his remains were consigned to the earth in Roxbury, with military honours. A widow and three children survived him. Like many others he suffered his private fortune to diminish while engaged in the service of his country; and although some relief was extended to his family by Congress, his pecuniary rewards, as in many other cases, bore no proportion to his public services. But his memory is embalmed in the hearts of his countrymen.

CHAPTER XV.

Condition of Vermont in 1783 — Continued prosperity — Federal constitution, 1788 — Adjustment of the difficulty with New York, 1790 — The close of the Continental Congress — The new Congress and its services — Prosperous condition of the country — Population of Vermont at different periods — Death of Colonel Ethan Allen — Remarks upon his character — Observations of Colonel Graydon respecting him — His personal appearance — His style of conversation — General Washington's opinion of him — Colonel Allen as a man of honour — His rebuke to the lawyer.

THE peace with Great Britain, in 1783, found Vermont in a very enviable position in some respects as compared with the states in the American Union. The boundaries of the new state had been tacitly defined and established, and the internal government was now proceeding as quietly and with as much benefit and advantage to the people as that of any other state on the continent. The laws were few, simple, and well-administered. Taxes were light, and the salaries of state officers were on a more frugal scale than in any other political community in the world. The danger of invasion, and the uncertainties and barbarities of war having ceased, the Vermont lands, the title being now in the state government, were rapidly taken up and settled by emigrants from other states. From this source a revenue was derived which tended still further to abate the pecuniary liabilities of the people in support of their institutions. The pastoral and happy state seemed to realize the dreams of political enthusiasts of a perfect commonwealth; and the backwoodsmen who had been buffeted by their more advanced neighbours, invited, repulsed, and trifled with, now locked with a sort of dignified pity on the factions and troubles which disturbed the Union, and rejoiced that they were not affected by them.

The immense debt—hopeless of liquidation as it then appeared—which had been contracted in the prosecution of the War of Independence, did not affect Vermont. Politically unrecognised, the urgent demands of Congress upon the states to furnish their quota, Vermont would not hear and need not heed. Her own troops, raised to defend her own territory, she was obliged to pay; but the finesse and policy of her managers, which postponed invasion by diplomacy, had rendered but a small army necessary. Under such circumstances we may well imagine that the people of Vermont had ceased to feel any solicitude to be admitted into the Union. There were still undecided questions—particularly as to land titles and jurisdictions; but a quarter of a century had accustomed them to this inconvenience, and the pause in the active proceedings of New York had rendered the evils more theoretical than actual.

Vermont escaped the discussion, in many of the states conducted with a great deal of acrimony, which attended the adoption of the Federal constitution. No doubt her leading men looked on, and her people debated the advantages and disadvantages of the proposed Federal Union under the new constitution, but it was as spectators and not as participants. When, by the Convention of 1787, the constitution was determined upon, and in that and the following year, eleven states came into the Union, South Carolina following in 1789, and Rhode Island in 1790, the inhabitants of Vermont perceived, in the workings of the new system, the promise of perpetuity and the prospect of relief from the public debt. They discovered, moreover, that the Federal government possessed a strength which contrasted favourably with the inefficiency of the old Congress and confederation, and were now again disposed to enter the Union.

The old opponent of Vermont, New York, was now not only willing but anxious that Vermont should come into the confederacy. The position of things had changed, and Vermont with her two senators could do New York and the northern interest better service than if her territory were an integral part of any other state, and could, therefore, add nothing to the weight of the Northern states in the Senate. The question of jurisdiction, long since tacitly relinquished, was now waived altogether, and the only point to be determined was in regard to the conflicting land-titles, and the claims of those adherents of New York who had been dispossessed and expelled from Vermont. Commissioners were appointed by the two states, who met and defined the boundary as claimed by Vermont, and agreed upon the sum of thirty thousand dollars, to be paid by Vermont to New York for the extinguishment of the disputed titles. These conditions, agreed upon by the commissioners, were ratified by the legislatures of the two states in 1790, and an end was thus put to a controversy which had lasted for twenty-six years. In reviewing the dispute, though we are compelled to admit that the Green Mountain Boys did many rude and lawless acts, we cannot but admire their sturdy resistance. They certainly were the oppressed party in the dispute; and the wisdom and courage with which they contended against superior power, and the firm adherence which they preserved, under their ungracious treatment, to the cause of freedom and their common country, are deserving of high praise. Their services were most important in bringing the struggle with Great Britain to a successful issue. In defending their territory, whether by arms or by artifice, they were defending the confederacy, and aiding the common cause, even while the treatment which they received from the Congress was discourteous, if not oppressive. But, as we have already remarked, it is rather wonderful that Congress effected so much, than that there should have been some cause of complaint; and it is only by closer reading than the common compendious histories of the Revolutionary period furnish, that we are enabled to do justice to that remarkable body, the Continental Congress.

The new Congress met in New York, in 1789, but it was not until April 6th, a month after the time appointed for assembling, that a quorum of members of the two houses came together. Their first duty was to count the votes for president and vice-president. Washington had sixty-nine votes, the whole number cast. By the constitution of the United States, as at first adopted, the candidate receiving the next highest number was declared vice-president. John Adams received thirty-four votes, and was elected. The labours of the first Congress are thus summed up by Hildreth, in his History of the United States, and a better review of their proceedings has not been given. "It was a body, next to the convention that framed the constitution, by far the most illustrious and remarkable in our post-revolutionary annals. On coming together, the new Congress had found the expiring government of the confederation without revenue, without credit, without authority, influence, or respect, at home or abroad; the state governments suffering under severe pecuniary embarrassments; and a large portion of the individuals who composed the nation overwhelmed by private debts. Commerce and industry, without protection from foreign competition, and suffering under all the evils of a depreciated and uncertain currency, exposed also to serious embarrassments from local jealousies and rivalries, were but slowly and painfully recovering from the severe dislocations to which, first, the War of the Revolution, and then the peace had subjected them. Even the practicability of carrying the new constitution into effect, at least without making the remedy worse than the disease, was seriously doubted, and stoutly denied by a powerful party having many able men among its leaders, and, numerically considered, including perhaps a majority of the people of the United States.

"In two short years a competent revenue had been provided, the duties imposed to produce it operating also to give to American producers a preference in the home market, and to secure to American shipping a like preference in American ports. The public debt, not that of the confederation only, but the great bulk of the state debts, had been funded, and the interest provided for, the public credit having been thus raised from the lowest degradation to a most respectable position. The very funding of this debt, and the consequent steady and increasing value thus conferred upon it, had given a new character to the currency, composed as it was, in a great measure, of the public securities; while steps had been taken to improve it still further by the establishment of a national bank. A national judiciary had been organized, vested with powers to guard the sanctity of contracts against stop laws, tender laws, and paper money. The practicability and efficiency of the new system had been as fully established as the experience of only two years would admit, and the nation thereby raised to a respectable position in its own eyes, and in those of foreign countries."

Such was the condition of things when, in 1791, Vermont, without a dissenting vote, was admitted into the Union. The little state came in on the tenth wave, having escaped all the eight years of trouble and doubt which intervened between the proclamation of peace and the adoption of the Federal constitution. Her membership of the confederacy commenced on the 4th of March, 1791. The first senators were Moses Robinson and Stephen R. Bradley; representatives, Nathaniel Niles and Israel Smith. Her Congressional delegates from that time to the present have been such as to do honour to the state they represented, and to command the respect of their associates in Congress. The number of representatives to which Vermont is entitled by the present appointment, is four. The population at the commencement of the Revolution was estimated at twenty thousand, and at the close at thirty thousand. The successive decennial enumerations of the inhabitants, from the date of the admission of the state into the Union, are as follows: 1791, 85,416; 1800, 154,465; 1810, 217,713; 1820, 235,764; 1830, 280,652; 1840, 281,948; 1850, 314,120. The ratio of increase, very large at the beginning, has become much reduced. This is a necessary consequence of the fact that the state contains an agricultural community; and of course its population must be less than where commerce and manufactures collect large bodies of inhabitants in a limited space.

Colonel Ethan Allen died in 1779, having lived to witness the termination of the contest with New York, in which he had borne so large a part from the commencement to the close. At the time of his death he was aged only fifty years, and many of his eccentric movements, as leader of the "Green Mountain Boys," may be placed to the account of youthful extravagance. But he was all his life through an eccentric man, quite as remarkable for his peculiarities as praiseworthy for his services. He was, unhappily, a sceptic in religion, and had an unfortunate habit of obtruding his opinions, not only in conversation but by printing them. So wild were some of his fancies, that the opinion has been maintained by many who had opportunity for judging, that his peculiarities were assumed in order to excite remark. He had the virtues and the follies which would naturally be looked for from the circumstances of his life. Colonel Graydon, who was his fellow-prisoner in New York, speaks in a kind and impartial manner of him. After quoting some of Allen's strangely violent language, Graydon says:

"Should this language seem too highly wrought, it should be remembered that few have ever more severely felt the hand of arbitrary power than Allen, and that he had but recently emerged from the provost guard, to which, for some alleged infringement of parole, he and Major O. H. Williams, a very gallant and distinguished officer, had been committed. Allen had been brought from Halifax to New York, and was admitted to parole when we were. His figure was that of a robust, large-framed man, worn down by confinement and hard fare; but he was now recovering his flesh and spirits, and a suit of blue clothes, with a gold-laced hat that had been presented to him by the gentlemen of Cork, enabled him to make a very passable appearance for a rebel colonel. He used to show a fracture in one of his teeth occasioned by his twisting off with it, in a fit of anger, the nail which fastened the bar of his hand-cuffs. I had become well acquainted with him, and have more than once heard him relate his adventures while a prisoner before being brought to New York, exactly corresponding in substance and language with the narrative he gave the public in 1779. I have seldom met with a man possessing a stronger mind, or whose mode of expression was more vehement and oratorical. His style was a singular compound of local barbarisms, scriptural phrases, and oriental wildness; and though unclassic, and sometimes ungrammatical, it was highly animated and forcible. * * * Notwithstanding that Allen might have had something of the insubordinate, lawless, frontier spirit in his composition, having been in a state of hostility with the government of New York before the Revolution, he appeared to me to be a man of generosity and honour, several instances of which occur in his publication, and one, not equivocal, came under my own observation. General Washington, speaking of him in an official letter, of May 12th, 1788, observes, with a just discrimination, that there was an original something in him which commanded admiration."

The incident referred to by Colonel Graydon is the following. Certain American officers, prisoners on parole, had been committed temporarily to close confinement. On their release, without the exaction of a new parole, they submitted the question to a board of officers whether they would not be justified in going away. "I forget," says Graydon, "who composed the board. I only recollect that Colonel Ethan Allen was one, and that his opinion was that of a man of honour, and a sound casuist. He admitted that they had a right to escape from their actual confinement, but that now the case was altered; and that, although no new parole had been given, yet the obligation of the former one should be considered as returning on their enlargement, and that they were under the same restraint, in point of honour, that they had been before their commitment to the provost. This was also the opinion of the board, and unanimously approved, as well by the gentlemen immediately interested as by others. I have mentioned this circumstance principally to show that Allen, however turbulent a citizen under the old regime, was not the vulgar ruffian that the New York royalists represented him." We may add another anecdote illustrative of Allen's sense of honour. A suit had been commenced against him on a note of hand. Allen employed a lawyer to procure a postponement of the judgment. The lawyer, as the easiest method to procure delay, denied his client's signature, that the difficulty of proving it might make the other party consent to a postponement. "Sir," shouted Allen, who happened to be in court, and came striding forward in a great passion— "Sir, I did not employ you to come here and *lie!* The note is good, the signature is *mine!* I only want time." The court and spectators were much amused at the quaint proceeding, and the plaintiff at once consented to a continuance.

Perfection is not to be looked for in humanity. But while we admire the virtues of those who have been distinguished benefactors of their country, we must not take license from their admitted good qualities to imitate their faults and follies. The troublous times which bring out strong men in a good point of view, give occasion also to irregularities, which in a quiet and peaceful era would not be tolerated. War is no school of the virtues; and we must weigh well the circumstances with which a man is surrounded, before we make up an opinion on his character.

CHAPTER XVI.

Vermont from 1791 to 1814 — Reservation of lands for religious and educational purposes — Foundation of Vermont school fund—University of Vermont — Donation from the state — Endowment by individual subscription — Liberality of Ira Allen — College buildings and library — Middlebury and Norwich colleges — Medical schools — Academies and common schools — Care of the early settlers for the education of their children — Its practical direction — Remarks of Dr. Williams — Ira Allen — Notices of his life — His History of Vermont — Governor Chittenden's quiet policy — Election of Governor Tichenor — Introduction of gubernatorial messages and replies by the legislature — Decided Federal majority — The Democrats elect their governor in 1807 — Tichenor re-elected in 1808 — The Democrats again successful in 1809 — Their candidate re-elected for five years — Party excitement increases — Declaration of war with Great Britain — Strong measures of the Democratic majority — Political revolution — Displacement of the Democrats — Election of Martin Chittenden — Repeal of the Democratic war measures — Capitulation of Hull — Destruction of stores at Plattsburg — Abortive attempt to invade Canada — Governor Chittenden recalls the Vermont militia — Battle of Lake Erie — Chippewa and Lundy's Lane — Battle of Plattsburg — Defeat and death of Captain Downie, and retreat of Sir George Prevost.

AMONG the excellent provisions of the Vermont constitution was one requiring public schools to be maintained in every town at the public expense. In every township grant made by the state of Vermont, one right was reserved for town, and one for county schools. In the grants made by Benning Wentworth, governor of New Hampshire, three rights were reserved, one for the Venerable Society for Propagating the Gospel, an English missionary association, one for a glebe for the Episcopal clergy, and one for the first settled clergyman, of whatever denomination he might be, as his private property, the design being to encourage the settlement of clergymen. By an act of the Vermont legislature, in 1794, the right of the Venerable Society, that body never having improved their grants, was applied to school purposes. From the proceeds of the school lands, and the lands added by the legislature as above

127

mentioned, originated the Vermont school fund, which now amounts to between two and three hundred thousand dollars. The state of Vermont also reserved two rights in her grants of townships for the support of the clergy, one for a parsonage, the other as a present to the first clergyman.

In addition to the common school provision, the people of Vermont, immediately after their admission into the Union, made provision for a university. The University of Vermont, at Burlington, was chartered in 1791, and went into operation in 1800. It had a donation of land from the state, amounting to fifty thousand acres, and was endowed by private subscription to the amount of $33,333. Nearly one-half of this sum was contributed by Ira Allen. The original college building, a large structure completed in 1801, was destroyed by fire in 1824, and finer buildings have been erected in its place. It has seven instructors and about one hundred and thirty students, and a library of about ten thousand volumes. The rental from its leased lands amounts to about $3,000 annually. Middlebury College, founded in 1800, is situated in the town from which it takes its name. It has the same number of professors as the University, a library of eight thousand volumes, and three college edifices. About one-third of its graduates have been clergymen. The Norwich College, chartered in 1834, makes the third large institution for education in the state. This is also a flourishing institution. It grew out of Captain Partridge's school, originally established in 1820. Its professorships are the same in number as the others, and it has the peculiarity of establishing no term for its collegiate course, the candidates for degrees being examined as to their qualifications. Besides these institutions there are in Vermont two medical schools, one at Castleton and one at Woodstock. The average attendance at these five institutions is about five hundred. There are fifty academies in the state, and about twenty-five hundred common schools.

From these statements it will appear that the wise forethought of the early settlers of Vermont has been well exhibited in its results. Dr. Williams, writing in 1794, while these educational advantages were as yet in the future, thus speaks of the character of the people, and their care of their children. "Among the customs which are universal among the people in all parts of the state, one that seems worthy of remark is the attention that is paid to the education of children. The aim of the parent is not so much to have his children acquainted with the liberal arts and sciences, but to have them all taught to read with ease and propriety, to write a plain and legible hand, and to have them acquainted with the rules of arithmetic so far as shall be necessary to carry on any of the most common and useful occupations of life. All the children are trained up to this kind of knowledge. They are accustomed from their earliest years to read the Holy Scriptures, the periodical publications, newspapers, and political pamphlets; to form some general acquaintance with the laws of their country, the proceedings of the courts of justice, of the general assembly of the state, and of Congress. Such a kind of education is common and universal in every part of the state. And nothing would be more dishonourable to the parents or to the children than to be without it. One of the first things the new settlers attend to is to procure a schoolmaster to instruct their children in the arts of reading, writing, and arithmetic. And where they are not able to procure an instructor, the parents attend to it themselves. No greater misfortune could attend a child than to arrive at manhood unable to read, write, and keep small accounts. He is viewed as unfit for the common business of the towns and plantations, and in a state greatly inferior to his neighbours. Every consideration joins to prevent so degraded and mortifying a state, by giving to every one the customary education and advantages. This custom was derived from the people of New England, and it has acquired greater force in the new settlements, where the people are apprehensive their children will have less advantages, and, of course, not appear equal to the children in the older towns."

We have mentioned Ira Allen as one of the most munificent benefactors of the Vermont University. This gentleman, the youngest of a family of eight, was the brother of the famous Ethan Allen, and, though less celebrated in romantic legends, was a most active and useful citizen. He was, with his brothers, among the earliest explorers of the territory of Vermont, and by judicious purchase became wealthy, when the lands which he had selected acquired value by the growth of the state. He was a distinguished actor in the events of the Revolution, as has already been recorded in these pages, and was connected with the affairs of the public through his life. He filled the offices of treasurer, member of the council, and major-general of the militia; and in the latter capacity had a trial, like his brother, of foreign imprisonment. Having purchased arms in England, in 1795, for the use of the state of Vermont, he was captured on his return, by a British vessel, and carried to

England on a charge of supplying the Irish, who were then in rebellion, with arms. After a litigation of eight years he obtained a verdict for damages, and returned to America. He wrote an historical memoir of Vermont, which, without quite the extravagance of his brother's style, has still some of its peculiarities. Other brothers of this family have been also prominent in the affairs of the state. Ira Allen died in Philadelphia, in 1814, in the sixty-third year of his age.

The affairs of the state of Vermont, from her admission into the Union to the death of Chittenden, in 1797, ran on in their quiet and even tenor. Governor Chittenden remained in office from 1778 to 1797, with the exception of one year. He was a man of moderate views in party politics as the line became drawn between the Federalist and Democratic parties, but inclined in his opinions to the latter or opposition side. But he sent no messages to the legislature at their annual assembly; and during the whole term which he held the office preserved the simplicity which had marked the commencement of his administration. His successor, Isaac Tichenor, elected by the legislature in 1797, (the people failing to elect,) introduced into Vermont the custom of the other states, and opened the legislature with a message, which was decided in its tone of approval of the administration of the elder Adams, then president, and, of course, distinctly placed the governor, and the large majority of the legislature which supported him, in the ranks of the Federal party. Mr. Tichenor continued in office until 1807, when the democratic party succeeded in electing their candidate, Israel Smith, but Governor Tichenor was again elected in 1808. In 1809 the Democrats again succeeded, and their candidate, Jonas Galusha, was re-elected annually, until 1813.

The proceedings of the legislature of Vermont were usually despatched in three to five weeks, and still remain shorter than those of the other states in the Union. There is less of private or special legislation; and the code of laws is brief yet comprehensive. But for the election of judges and other civil officers, which is part of the duty of the Vermont legislature, there would be scarce an opportunity for excitement; and even on this subject there is not much, as the emoluments of office are not such as to tempt cupidity. The annual message, introduced by Governor Tichenor, and the reply which it was the early custom of the assembly to make, were, in the early days of the state, sometimes the occasion of some heat. This custom was discontinued in 1816. At the end of one of these stormy debates a member gravely proposed a resolution, seriously recommending that the governor should not thereafter make a formal address. The resolution was not carried, but had its effect in making some succeeding gubernatorial addresses less political and more practical. Addresses to the president of the United States were another theme of dispute. One was voted to the elder Adams, two to Jefferson, and one to Monroe.

The declaration of war against Great Britain found the Democratic or war party in the ascendent in the Vermont legislature, with a governor, Jonas Galusha, of the same political opinions. In his annual message, Governor Galusha urged the assembly to second the measures of the general government and the assembly responded in the same spirit. A resolution was passed in the following strong language. "We pledge ourselves to each other and to our government, that with our individual exertions, our example and influence, we will support our government and country in the present contest, and rely upon the great Arbiter of events for a favourable result." The vote upon this resolution was one hundred and twenty-eight to seventy-nine; and in the same spirit, the minority protesting, the legislature proceeded to enact some strong laws in aid of the general cause. Intercourse between the people of the state and Canada was forbidden under a penalty of $1,000, and seven years imprisonment. A stringent drafting law was passed, thirty dollars bounty was offered to volunteers, and the pay of the Vermont militia in the service of the United States was doubled by as much more from the state as was paid by the United States. The person and property of soldiers was exempted from attachment while they were in service. To meet the presumed expenses of these measures, an additional tax of one per cent. was levied.

While these measures were very effective in bringing a force into the field, they operated in another direction in quite as efficient a manner. At the election in 1813 the majority of the assembly was precisely reversed. The actual burden of taxation—more tangible than mere words and resolves—produced such an overturn as put the Democrats in the protesting ranks. There was no choice of governor by the people. Martin Chittenden, the Federal candidate, was elected after several trials, by a small majority. The governor's speech, and the answer to it, were in strong condemnation of the war and the measures of the government. Seventy-five democratic members

131

of the legislature "protested," and their protest was entered on the journal. The Democratic officers were removed, and the laws above mentioned as passed during the preceding session were repealed. Party spirit reached its climax of bitterness and anger. Opprobrious names were applied, social relations were interrupted, and it seemed almost as if civil war was impending.

While these party evolutions were performing in Vermont, war had already commenced with Great Britain—and most disastrously. Detroit, with a large portion of the American territory in the then "North-west," fell into the hands of the British, in August, 1812, by the capitulation of General Hull; and perhaps this event, which was appealed to by those opposed to the war, as an illustration of the folly of it, had no small influence in defeating the war party in Vermont, and the events of 1812 and 1813 on Lake Champlain had not a much better moral effect. Two armed American sloops, the Eagle and the Growler, in the pursuit of some British gunboats, fell into the hands of the enemy, June 2d, 1812. One of them, the Eagle, sunk within musket-shot of the Canadian shore, and the other, the Growler, being prevented from retreating by a strong southerly wind, was compelled to strike. A hundred prisoners were, in this affair, taken by the British. On the 30th of July these American sloops, in the charge of their new masters, paid a visit to Plattsburg, where they destroyed some military stores, estimated to be worth about $25,000. They also captured some small trading vessels, and destroyed other property. These indications of an intention to make Lake Champlain the scene of military operations, turned the attention of the United States government to that quarter. A naval force was equipped, mounting forty-eight guns, which was in the following year doubled. But no naval operations took place upon the lake during this season—the British, overawed by a superior force, declining an engagement. The winter was employed, on both sides, in building and refitting naval armaments, which were during the next year to furnish one of the most spirited pages in the history of naval warfare.

The northern army of the United States, under command of General Hampton, made unsuccessful attempts to enter Canada by two different routes, but retired into winter quarters at Plattsburg without having effected any thing, except to discover that to force their way into Canada, in this direction, would be an enterprise costing more in blood and treasure than any advantage of success would compensate for. The most curious result of the

132

campaign was the surprise and capture of one hundred and one British soldiers, by one hundred and two Americans, at St. Amand's. Great excitement grew out of an act of Governor Chittenden's. A brigade of Vermont militia had been detailed by the predecessor of Governor Chittenden into the service of the United States. This brigade Governor Chittenden recalled by proclamation, denying the legality of such a draft, except to execute the laws of the Union, to suppress insurrection, or to repel invasion. Neither of these three emergencies existed in the present case. The officers of the brigade refused obedience, and made a written protest against the proclamation. But as it was issued within a few days of the time when the militia were entitled to their discharge, and after the army had retired to winter quarters, the difficulty was adjusted by the discharge of the militia.

But while little of moment had occurred on Lake Champlain, Lake Erie had been the scene of the brilliant victory of Capt. Perry, and the command of the lake was now, and remained during the war in the hands of the Americans. The British made no serious efforts to recover their ascendency. Michigan, lost by the surrender of Hull, was restored to the United States, and the northern frontier was relieved of the dangers with which Hull's disaster had seemed to threaten it. The territorial government of Michigan was reorganized. The vessels captured by Perry were used as transports, and General Harrison's troops were conveyed to the Canada side. Pursuing Procter, the English general, who had twice invaded Ohio, the battle of the Thames restored the confidence of the American forces. Procter lost all his ammunition and baggage, and narrowly escaped himself. The American force returned triumphant, but without any attempt at a permanent occupation of Canada.

Early in the spring of 1814, the old war-path on Lake Champlain began to resume its interest. General Wilkinson added the testimony of his experience to the fact that no successful invasion could be attempted from either side of the Canada line upon the other. Advancing with four thousand men along the west side of Lake Champlain, he attempted to enter Canada, but was repulsed at the British outposts, and returned to Plattsburg. In July of the same year General Brown invaded Canada from Buffalo, and the battles of Chippewa and Lundy's Lane, while they exhibited the bravery of the American forces, again demonstrated that the permanent occupation of any part of Canada by the United States troops was an impossibility. The burning of towns and villages on either frontier, and the most barbarous exhibitions of partizan anger, were the aspects in which war was usually presented between Canada and the Northern states. From the previous intercourse and neighbourhood attachments of the parties, hostilities had all the bad characteristics of civil war—the most inhuman description of warfare.

A ship, a schooner, a brig, and several gunboats were built under the superintendence of Captain McDonough, during the winter and spring of 1814. They were constructed on the borders of Otter Creek, and the operations of the campaign were opened by an effort of the enemy to destroy the flotilla while yet incomplete. The invading force was, however, repulsed by the batteries at the mouth of the creek, and by the Vermont militia, and returned without effecting any thing. Nothing of moment occurred until the month of September, when the British naval and land forces made an advance upon Plattsburg. The fort was garrisoned by General Macomb, with a force of about fifteen hundred effective men. The flotilla of Captain McDonough carried eighty-six guns, and was manned by eight hundred and twenty men. Sir George Prevost, the English commander-in-chief, had a force of twelve thousand, and the English flotilla, commanded by Captain Downie, carried ninety-six guns, and was manned by one thousand and fifty men. The American fleet chose a position, and waited at anchor for the approach of the enemy. On the morning of the 11th of September, the British fleet entered the harbour of Plattsburg in the full confidence of victory.

Great efforts had been made, and with good success, to reinforce General Macomb in his position at Plattsburg. Expresses had been sent into Vermont, and Governor Chittenden called earnestly upon the people to volunteer for the defence of Plattsburg. The fort was in full view of the fleet, and the soldiers waited in a fever of impatience for the double assault, by land and by water. General Prevost moved slowly to the attack, apparently waiting for the commencement of the naval action as the signal for the land assault.

The two larger vessels of the American flotilla, were the Saratoga, twenty-six guns, and the Eagle, twenty. The Eagle opened the engagement. In his Naval History, Cooper gives a very interesting anecdote respecting the commencement of the engagement. A few minutes passed in the solemn and silent expectation that, in a disciplined ship, always precedes a battle. Suddenly the Eagle discharged, in quick succession, four guns in broadside. In clearing the decks of the Saratoga some hen-coops were thrown overboard, and the poultry had been permitted to run at large. Startled by the reports of the guns, a young cock flew upon a gun-slide, clapped his wings and crowed. At this animating sound the men spontaneously gave three cheers. This little occurrence relieved the breathing time between preparation and the combat, and it had a powerful influence upon the known tendencies of the seamen. Still Captain McDonough did not give the order to commence, for it was apparent that the fire of the Eagle, which vessel still continued to engage, was useless. As soon, however, as it was seen that her shot told, Captain McDonough himself sighted one of the Saratoga's long twenty-fours, and the gun was fired. This shot is said to have struck the Confiance near the outer hawsehole, and to have passed the length of her deck, killing and wounding several men, and carrying away the steering wheel.

The English vessels came up in gallant style, and anchored in the face of this cannonade. The Confiance carried thirty-seven guns, thirty-one of which were long twenty-fours, and she had been built in defiance of any force which could be opposed to her. Could this vessel once get the desired position, it was considered that she would decide the fate of the day. But she was handled too roughly in coming up; and when at last she came to anchor, it was at an unfavourable distance from the American line. Her first broadside told terribly on the Saratoga. Forty men were killed and wounded by this single discharge.

The engagement now became general, and after an action of about three hours, not an English flag floated in the bay—all were lowered. The Confiance, terribly crippled, and the commander of the flotilla killed, being the first to strike. The smaller vessels followed the example; but, by a curious accident, related by Cooper, the British galleys escaped. They were drifting with their flags down, ready to be taken possession of as prizes, when an accidental discharge of a gun on board the Confiance was mistaken for a signal, and the English galleys made off slowly and irregularly, as if distrusting their own liberty. There was not a vessel among the larger ones whose masts would bear a sail, and the men from the American galleys were wanted at the pumps of the prizes to keep them afloat. No accurate report of the killed and wounded has been obtained. The British loss must have exceeded two

135

hundred and fifty killed and wounded, and among the former were Captain Downie and three lieutenants. The American loss was one hundred and ten killed and wounded, and among the former were lieutenants Gamble and Stansbury.

Sir George Prevost, who had hardly commenced the action on shore when the fate of the fleet was decided, made a most unmilitary and precipitate retreat, leaving all his baggage and military stores, and losing in killed, wounded, prisoners and deserters, over twenty-five hundred men. The loss of the Americans in the land engagement did not exceed one hundred and fifty.

CHAPTER XVII.

Re-election of Governor Chittenden — His annual address — Vermont refuses to send delegates to the Hartford Convention — The victors of Plattsburg complimented for their services — Grant of land to McDonough — Treaty of Ghent — Review of the war — Honesty of the war and peace parties — Statistics of Vermont — Population, agriculture, manufactures — Cotton, wool, and iron — The lumber business — Miscellaneous statistics — Inland navigation — Railroads — Banks — Benevolent institutions —State income and expenditure — Religious denominations — Closing remarks.

WITH the victory of Plattsburg, the war, so far as Vermont was concerned, was at an end. The Vermont volunteer soldiery had highly distinguished themselves by the alacrity with which they responded to the call of their country, forgetful of all party differences. Governor Chittenden, who was re-elected by the legislature, by a majority of twenty-nine votes, in his annual address, paid a high compliment to the soldiers who had repulsed the enemy. He said they had taught them the "mortifying lesson that the soil of freedom will not bear the tread of hostile feet with impunity," and he pronounced their achievements "unsurpassed in the records of naval and military warfare." But he manfully adhered to his opinion of the war, and declared that he "conscientiously disapproved of it as unnecessary, unwise, and hopeless in all its offensive operations." In the same address he adverted to the complaints which had been made that he did not order out the militia for the defence of Plattsburg, instead of calling for volunteers. He said that as no portion of the militia of Vermont had been detached by the president, the call upon them as volunteers was the only mode in which efficient and timely aid could be afforded. The house returned a dignified and respectful answer, avoiding such topics as would have elicited debate. Indeed, the pressure from without, and the actual invasion of the country, seemed to have calmed the angry waters of strife.

An invitation from Massachusetts to send delegates to the Hartford Convention, was unanimously declined by the same legislature which had elected a Federal governor. And this Federal governor, it should be noticed, was a man of character and decided opinions. In Congress he had distinguished himself as the opponent of the embargo; and as governor, during his first term, he issued the proclamation mentioned in the last chapter, for which there was a proposition made in Congress to instruct the attorney-general to impeach him. The Massachusetts legislature supported him in a series of resolutions. The legislature of Pennsylvania denounced him, and the legislature of New Jersey characterized him as a "maniac governor." Little Vermont has had the fortune to make a sensation in the confederacy altogether greater than her importance in regard to population and wealth. But her sturdy independence has done good service in vindicating the rights of small states to be respected, and in practically defending that wise theory of the Union, which bases the privileges of the commonwealths in the Union, not on their power, but on their rights.

At this session of the legislature, resolutions were passed highly complimentary to General Macomb, to Captain McDonough, and their officers and men, and to General Strong and the Vermont volunteers. To Captain McDonough, the legislature presented a farm on Cumberland Head, in sight of the scene of his victory. Other compliments and gifts were made him by Congress, and different states and towns.

In December, 1814, the plenipotentiaries of the respective nations signed a treaty of peace at Ghent, between the United States and Great Britain. In reviewing the events of the war, so far as they have entered into the history of Vermont, or have been necessary to illustrate our narrative, we have endeavoured to be impartial. In the Revolutionary War there was but one American party. Whoever opposed that war befriended the claims of a foreign power. But in the last war there could be an honest difference of opinion without prejudice to the patriotism of the holders. In the heat of party excitement it was natural to charge, and even to suspect improper motives. But as time gives us more impartial views, and removes the exasperation of party feeling, we must concede to the opponents, as well as to the friends of the war, true patriotism. And we must concede also that many of the selfish and designing had no higher object than their own advantage in opposition or in defence of the measure. We should tremble for the republic if, in this century, the people should be found unanimously in favour of war with any people, or under any circumstances. At this distance of time we can perceive that so far as any war can be conducive to the advantage of a nation, this war was to the United States in some important particulars. But we are free from the losses, the sufferings, and the perils which entered into the estimate of contemporaries; and we, too, in a time of peace, can condemn all war as unchristian and unnecessary without being suspected of treachery to our country. Could not those who honestly held the same opinion then, hold it without a treacherous wish or purpose?

At the election in 1815, it was found that the democratic party was again in the ascendency. And as party spirit died away with the removal of causes of excitement, the words Federalist and Democrat ceased to be a rallying cry, or to be applied as terms of opprobrium. It would be neither profitable nor interesting to follow all the party contests which have taken their rise from temporary or local causes, or the preference of the people for particular men. Suffice it of the noble and patriotic state of Vermont to say, that she has ever shown herself practically republican.

We have stated the increase of population in a preceding chapter, the present population of the state being 314,120. A few statistics of agricultural and other productions, will exhibit what this population is capable of effecting. The number of acres of land under cultivation, in 1850, was 2,322,923; value of farming implements and machinery, $2,774,959; of live stock, $11,292,748; of home-made manufactures, $261,589. The number of bushels of wheat raised, was 493,666; of Indian corn, 1,625,776. The number of pounds of wool produced was 3,492,087; of butter, 12,128,095; of cheese, 6,755,006; of maple sugar, 5,159,641; tons of hay, 763,579. The cotton manufacture of the state is carried on by nine establishments, in which a capital of $202,500 is invested. The annual value of all raw material is $114,115; of products, $196,100; operatives, 250; monthly wages, $3,321. In the woollen manufacture there is a capital of $886,300, invested in seventy-two establishments, using in a year raw material to the amount of $830,684, and producing an annual value of $1,579,161. The number of operatives is 1493, receiving monthly wages amounting to $25,100. The capital invested in iron works in 1850, was $325,920; raw material, $206,972; value of products,

$692,817. These statistics do not include, of course, all the products of the industry of the people; nor is it possible, by the most careful estimates and inquiries, to obtain any thing more than an approximation to the whole productions of the state. Besides the great staples of agriculture mentioned above, the smaller ones are produced in abundance, although the state is better adapted to grazing than to grain.

The lumber business annually produces about $400,000, and about seven hundred tons of pot and pearl ashes; its orchard products are $200,000; poultry, $200,000; hats, caps, and bonnets, $70,000; bricks and lime, $300,000; marble and granite, $70,000. The chief supply of black marble used in the United States comes from the quarries on Lake Champlain; and some beautiful varieties of dove-coloured, white and clouded marbles are found in Vermont. Vessels for lake and river navigation are annually built, to the value of about $80,000, and these are employed in the trade of the state with New York and Canada on Lake Champlain, and the rivers and canals with which the waters of that lake are connected. And we may here observe that this important avenue to the interior of the country, which has during two wars been the path of foreign invasion, is now guarded by fortifications which can easily be made impregnable. Rouse's Point, near the Canadian line, has fortifications which cannot be passed by water. At the close of the last war the United States government caused this point to be fortified, but the awkward discovery was made that the point was not within the United States boundary, and the work was therefore abandoned. By the treaty of Washington, negotiated in 1842, by Mr. Webster and Lord Ashburton, Rouse's Point was obtained for the United States, thus securing the key of Lake Champlain; and the state of Vermont obtained also about sixty-one thousand acres which would have been left, by the true parallel of 45°, on the Canada side of the line.

Vermont has her share of railroads, which intersect the state in all desirable and profitable directions, in length over four hundred miles. Less accidents have occurred upon them than on any other roads in the United States. Her banking capital is about a million and a half. She has a state institution for the insane, and other public buildings, on a scale commensurate with her wants, and adapted to modern views of philanthropy. She has no town with a population exceeding five thousand, and thus escapes the difficulties in enforcing wholesome general laws—a disadvantage which large cities impose as a counterpoise to their benefits. Her annual state income is about one hundred thousand dollars; and her expenses fall so far short of this, that although she has had temporary debts for specific purposes they were soon extinguished.

The preponderating religious denominations are the Congregationalists, Baptists, and Methodists. Next to these come the Episcopalians. The smaller denominations are also represented, and the regard paid to the Sabbath and to religious instructions and institutions is general and evident in the character of the people. Printing presses, periodicals, daily, semi-weekly, weekly, and monthly, abound in the true New England proportion; and books, with the Vermont imprint, chiefly Bibles, historical works, and other standards, are found throughout New England.

Montpelier has been for nearly half a century the capital of the state—the legislature in its first years being migratory. The State House is a beautiful building, in a mixed style of Grecian architecture, and, with the other public buildings, is worthy of the state. The State House has, as trophies, the four cannon captured by Stark in the Battle of Bennington. These cannon tell the story of two wars. They were lost by Hull at the surrender of Detroit, recaptured by the Americans at the taking of Fort George, and remained many years unclaimed and forgotten by Vermont, in the arsenal at Washington. There they were observed, with their inscription, by Hon. Henry Stevens; and, at his request, restored by Congress to the gallant state, on the soil where they were captured. Another memorial of her services and sufferings in the wars of the Union is found in her military pension list, which, even as late as 1840, numbered 1,320 out of 291,948 inhabitants, a proportion greatly diminished from the earlier pension roll.

Such are some of the facts in the history and statistics of Vermont. We have given without partiality the narrative of her progress, from the early days when resistance to wrong exposed her rude patriots to error, down to her present quiet and orderly condition. The services she has rendered to the Union as a frontier state, entitle her to our highest gratitude; for while in war she was distinguished in arms, in peace she has proved herself equal to the maintenance of a delicate and troublesome position. She sheltered the fugitives during the Canadian rebellion without compromising the country; and her people followed the natural sympathies of republicans, without doing violence to her duty, as one of the United States, to a friendly government. The stranger from Europe, who enters the United States at the great commercial sea-ports, with their half foreign aspects, has not the advantages of observation which those possess, who find the Genius of America "at home" in Vermont, as soon as they cross her threshhold. And through this entrance the American may proudly welcome those who come hither seeking a home, or desiring to see the wonderful political and social experiment of the nineteenth century—a government strong without antique precedents— supported by citizens of distinct state sovereignties, with great local diversities of character and pursuits, yet moving harmoniously together by a common vigorous impulse to maintain the national honour and the integrity of the Federal compact.

THE END.

CPSIA information can be obtained
at www.ICGtesting.com
Printed in the USA
BVHW040233080223
657828BV00014B/562

9 781396 320095